# The People's Republic of China: 1978–1990

D. Gale Johnson

An International Center for Economic Growth Publication

ICS Press
San Francisco, California

Publication signifies that the Center believes a work to be a competent treatment worthy of public consideration. The findings, interpretations, and conclusions of a work are entirely those of the author and should not be attributed to ICEG, its affiliated organizations, its board of overseers, or organizations that support ICEG.

Inquiries, book orders, and catalogue requests should be addressed to ICS Press, 243 Kearny Street, San Francisco, California 94108. Telephone: (415) 981-5353; Fax: (415) 986-4878.

---

**Library of Congress Cataloging-in-Publication Data**

Johnson, D. Gale (David Gale), 1916–
The People's Republic of China: 1978–1990 / D. Gale Johnson.
p. cm. — (Country studies; 8)
"An International Center for Economic Growth publication."
Includes bibliographical references.
ISBN 1–55815–122–2 (pbk.)
1. Agriculture and state—China. 2. Agriculture—Economic aspects—China. 3. China—Economic policy—1976– 4. China—Economic conditions—1976– I. Title. II. Series: Country studies (San Francisco, Calif.); 8.
HD 1698.C52J64 1990
338.1'851'09045—dc20

90–40204
CIP

*To Helen,*
*who shared her life with me for more than fifty years*

# Contents

# List of Tables

# Preface

This study of economic reforms in the People's Republic of China is the eighth in the ICEG series of Country Studies, which evaluate the broad effects of both macro- and microeconomic policies in developed and developing countries.

D. Gale Johnson's analysis of the economic reforms attempted and implemented in China begins with a brief history of the economic system from the first years after the Communist Revolution in 1949 through the Great Famine, industrialization, and the Cultural Revolution.

A crucial goal of the reforms has been the improvement of agricultural production and distribution. Johnson describes the successful results of some of the reforms as well as the reasons others have failed—the biases inherent in Chinese policies, for example: they include an urban bias that is reflected in subsidies to urban families for food, housing, and transportation; a bias that favors investment over consumption; and a bias favoring coastal residents and industries over those in the vast interior.

Johnson continues with a more detailed discussion of the complex agricultural and urban industrial reforms since 1978 and their effects on output, employment, prices, and living standards. He provides a fascinating look at the contrasts between urban and rural life in today's China as well as policy suggestions that might improve the lot of the average Chinese citizen.

Professor Johnson is one of the most distinguished agricultural economists of the past fifty years. His countributions to theory, policy, teaching, and administration have earned him well-deserved and ample recognition. We are pleased to publish this important contribution.

Nicolás Ardito-Barletta
General Director
International Center for Economic Growth

Panama City, Panama
November 1990

# Author's Preface

At the outset I want to make it clear that I do not consider myself a "China expert." I am an agricultural economist who began reading and writing about Soviet agriculture nearly four decades ago. I never intended, however, to specialize in its study; as time went by, I gradually extended my interests to agriculture in the other centrally planned economies, especially those in Eastern Europe.

In addition to my interest in socialist agricultures, my interest in the relationship between the growth rates of the world's food supply and demand over time induced me to add the People's Republic of China to the list of agricultures that I wanted to learn more about. Contrary to the conventional wisdom as expressed in the national news media, I have argued for about a quarter century that the food supply situation has improved, is improving, and will continue to improve in the low-income or developing countries. Yet, obviously, such a view cannot be held with confidence without some knowledge about what is occurring in China with its fifth of the world's population.

But perhaps the most important factor in my interest in Chinese agricultures was the decision of my daughter, Kay Ann Johnson, to choose China as her area of geographic specialization. Because she speaks Mandarin, she has been a most useful contributor to the education of her mother and father on the four trips that the three of us have made together to China. She also has been an important source of ideas and often induces me to rethink positions that I have come to accept. Her primary research interest has been, first, how the Communist Revolution affected the status of rural women and, second, how the lives of women have been influenced by the rural reforms that have occurred since 1978. Thus, her interests and mine have had much in common.

My understanding of Chinese reforms stems from the approximately six months I have spent in China since 1980, spread over a series of visits. On each visit I met with local officials in rural areas and from these visits gleaned a considerable part of the illustrative material contained in this publication. I also have had the privilege of working closely with several students from China and I have learned much from each of them. Moreover, a number of economists from China who spent extended periods of time at the University of Chicago were generous in sharing their views with me. Although I do not read or speak Chinese, I have had access to a growing body of material available in English, including extensive translations from the Foreign Broadcast Information Service, such publications as the *China Daily* and *Beijing Review,* and the English-language publications of the government of China. Finally, I have had the help of students who searched and translated the relevant Chinese publications.

In this monograph, I seek to provide a reasonably interesting analysis of what has been a remarkable effort to significantly reform a large and complex economy. I also hope to leave readers with an understanding of, first, why reform was believed to be essential and what some of the major reform measures were; second, why some reforms failed to achieve their objectives while others were remarkably successful; and, third, what the consequences of some of the more important reforms were. Finally, I describe the further reforms required to meet the overall reform objectives.

Until June 1989 I had been disturbed by the prospect of preparing a manuscript that dealt with an ever-changing scene without knowing what the next month or season would bring. The tragic events in Tiananmen Square provided a shocking end to an era. Even if the economic reforms continue apace, it is likely for a considerable time that discussions by Chinese scholars and officials will lack much of their past vigor and frankness. Critical discussions of the shortcomings and problems of the reforms are unlikely to appear in the press and scholarly journals in the near future. Can we trust the official information from a government that tried to tell the world that what hundreds of millions of people witnessed simply did not happen? It will be some time before confidence in the word of that government can be rebuilt. Taking these and other factors into account, I end my story quite deliberately with mid-1989. I make a number of suggestions, however, about what could be done to improve the economic circumstances of the people of China in the hope that such ideas, from whatever source, will be of interest to a future and more humane Chinese government.

# CHAPTER 1

# Background of Economic Reform in the People's Republic of China

It is commonly held that the agenda for economic reforms in the People's Republic of China was set in 1978, with implementation occurring in 1979, but some attention should be given to the period from Mao Zedong's death in 1976 to 1978. During that short period, economic plans duplicated most of the serious errors of certain earlier periods, particularly extremely high rates of investment and overheating of the economy through the continued centralization of its control and direction. First, however, it is useful to examine some of the major economic and social developments that have occurred since the Communist Revolution in 1949. Major emphasis will be given to the two decades following 1957, with some emphasis on the period of recovery and the First Five-Year Plan.

Rural rather than urban reforms will receive more attention here because rural reforms have affected 75–80 percent of the population directly and, through improvement in output and its distribution, have affected the rest of the population indirectly. Another reason is that urban and industrial reforms were still carried out very much on a trial-and-error basis as of mid-1989. This is not to say that the urban economy has stagnated over the past decade, but nothing approaching a systematic reform structure has appeared and endured. A final reason for emphasizing rural reforms is that with the introduction of the household responsibility system and the abolition of the commune, numerous individuals who had great authority lost much of that authority, at least temporarily. While there are problems that must be solved to achieve a high level of agricultural productivity and efficiency, some disquieting efforts to recollectivize agriculture are evident—but more on this later.

### Three Biases

Economic policies since the Communist Revolution—and the policies of the past decade are no exception—have exhibited three major biases that have had significant effects on the welfare of the Chinese people. The first and most striking is the urban bias, which has been pervasive over the past four decades. It has been and is represented by substantially higher per capita expenditures on consumption goods in urban than in rural areas, with the differential widening until 1979. Even with their much higher incomes, urban families have been given ever-increasing subsidies over the past decade to prevent increases in the prices of grain and vegetable oils from being reflected in prices paid by urban consumers and to cover the estimated costs of the relatively recent increases in the retail prices of fruits, vegetables, and meats. These subsidies, which now account for about a third of the central government's expenditures, go solely to urban consumers and a small number of employees of state agencies who live in rural areas. Urban consumers pay little or nothing for their housing, while rural families must pay the full cost of building and maintaining their houses. Urban transportation is heavily subsidized, while rural transportation is not; in fact, tens of thousands of rural villages are not even served by a road.

The urban bias is also evident in numerous comments that one hears from educated urban residents. The most irritating comment is that farm people—the peasants—do not deserve as much in the way of material goods as urban residents. Thus, not only does the disparity between urban and rural residents exist in fact, but in the opinion of many intellectuals and other urban residents such a large disparity is quite proper.

A related bias is that farm people should do the difficult and dirty work when they move to the cities. A recent report by the official Chinese news agency dealt with the issue of regulating farm labor, especially for rural workers seeking jobs in the cities (FBIS-CHI-89-074, April 19, 1989, 40). Two sentences from the report need no further interpretation: "Cities, too, need farmer workers, for there the dirty, tiring, and hard manual jobs have no one to do them. For instance, in Beijing, the city's textile industry needs thousands of farmers to do the hard manual jobs, and the city's urban engineering bureau can also use 1,000 such workers each year." In a story from the *People's Daily* about farmers who left the land to go to the cities, it was noted that "in cities, they usually take dirty, hard, harmful and risky jobs which urban dwellers shun" (FBIS-CHI-89-178, September 15, 1989, 37).

The second bias is an investment one, evident in a consistent de-emphasis of current consumption in favor of investment. It seems almost unconscionable that in a country with as low a per capita income as China's a third or more of the national income has been invested in some years. At times much of this investment has gone into projects having little lasting value or contributing minimally to productivity. Remarkably, this bias has persisted even when concerted efforts have been made to limit the amount of investment. The inflation of 1987–89, for example, stemmed largely from the failure to curb the availability of credit for investment, including construction projects. In fact, the investment bias seems at times to be systemic.

The third bias is the coastal area bias, represented in recent years by the failure to narrow the wide income gap between residents of the eastern coastal areas and those of the western interior areas. Although Mao did shift investments to the interior areas, which had some effect on incomes, the primary objective appeared to be meeting national security needs. The reforms of the past decade have not been effective in reducing the income disparities in the rural areas; if anything, the disparities have widened slightly. The reforms directly affecting agriculture—for example, the change in the incentive systems and the increases in output prices—have improved incomes of those fully engaged in agriculture, but the largest increases in incomes in rural areas have gone generally to those who have found a profitable nonfarm economic activity in commerce, transportation, construction, or industry. Consequently, in rural areas at a considerable distance from major cities, the benefits of rural reforms, while significant in increasing what had been a very low real income, have been somewhat more modest than the gains realized where there are alternatives to continued full-time involvement in farming.

These three biases should have merited the serious attention of policy makers, yet it is not obvious how they can be addressed effectively without drastic changes in some firmly held policies and a major reallocation of investment away from the current large urban areas and the coastal region to the interior. One approach to minimizing the urban bias would be to permit migration from rural to urban areas, but this has been and is now quite firmly controlled, although less so in recent years. The large income differences between urban and rural areas persist because it is virtually impossible for rural residents to change their official residence to a large urban area. One may actually reside in an urban area but without access to subsidized cereals, medical care, or the many other benefits accorded the official urban resident.

Knowledge of these biases will facilitate understanding the historical development of the Chinese economy and the policies followed by the government and the Communist party. Thus, what in other settings might be difficult to understand may be more readily absorbed if these three biases are kept in mind.

## Brief History of the Economic System

In the following brief history of the economic system that was the subject of the reform process begun in 1979, it will become clear that between 1949 and 1978 there was no so-called normal extended period of time during which any consistent program of policies reached equilibrium. Broken commitments, irrational responses, politically induced and fostered civil disruptions, and attempted palace revolts were scattered about the historical landscape. Twists and turns, seemingly based upon whims or gross misinformation, were widely evident. What is clear is that Chairman Mao's quixotic behavior prevented a fair test of what might have been accomplished by socialism in China. This is not to say that many Westerners would have been greatly impressed by what might have been achieved, but certainly hundreds of millions of Chinese would not have had imposed upon them a quarter century of uncertainty, hardship, misery, and repeated visitations of famine. The irrationality of what happened in Beijing in June 1989 did not differ significantly from some of Mao's more bizarre behavior.

**The first years.** The Communist Revolution of 1949 was followed from 1949 to 1952 by a period of recovery and substantial progress toward a return to normality after more than a decade of occupation by the Japanese civil war. Agricultural production may well have returned to its probable peak level of the mid-1930s. Official data indicate that agricultural output increased by almost 50 percent during the three years and, given its low level in 1949, such a large increase may well have occurred.

The First Five-Year Plan (1953–1957) is generally considered to have been a significant economic success; national income grew at an estimated annual rate of 9 percent. Agricultural output, in constant prices, grew at an annual rate of 4.5 percent, representing a combination of continued recovery from war and revolution and the effective agricultural policies that were followed.

Land reform had been completed by 1952. Approximately a third of the land had been transferred to peasant owners in the liberated areas as of 1949, and the remaining two-thirds had been subject to land reform during the next three years. At the conclusion of the land reform process in 1952 nearly 100 million individual farms were owner operated, and families had what most must have considered to be secure titles or rights to the land they were farming. But agriculture was collectivized in the winter of 1955–56; farm families found their independent status short-lived. Most Chinese families probably had had little familiarity with the fate of peasants in the Soviet Union who also had been given title to land only to be forced into collective and state farms in little more than a decade. Chinese farm families lost what many of them had fought for and had been promised. It took less than five years for most of their aspirations to be dashed. Mao moved much more quickly than Stalin to take from farmers what they had been given. According to the distinguished economist Xue Muqiao (1981, 35):

> The socialist transformation of China's agriculture was completed at a high speed. After the completion of agrarian reform, the Party Central Committee decided to "strike while the iron is hot" by following it up with a mutual aid and co-operation (collectivization) movement in agriculture. . . . The Party Central Committee had planned to complete agricultural co-operation in 15 years, but things came to a head in 1955.

He noted that only 2 percent of households were in cooperatives in 1954 and just 14 percent in 1955, but by the end of 1956, 96 percent had voluntarily chosen to give up their land, machinery, and livestock and join the cooperatives. According to Justin Lin (1990), a significant degree of voluntarism accompanied the formation of these cooperatives, but many farmers later withdrew, taking their land, equipment, and livestock with them and causing a considerable number of cooperatives to collapse. The rapidity with which these cooperatives were formed leaves one with a strong impression that considerable coercion had to have been applied in many, if not most, villages.

Cooperatives had an average of 200 families or somewhat more than 300 workers. The more than 500,000 cooperatives existing in 1957 were forcibly combined one year later to create about a tenth as many communes. The communes were authoritarian institutions, concentrating enormous power in their leaders. They combined both governmental (political) and economic power in one institution. As Xue wrote (1981, 36):

> A "communist wind" was stirred up, whereby equalitarianism prevailed and human and material resources were transferred without regard to the actual collectives to which they belonged. All this naturally dampened the enthusiasm of the peasants and cadres at the grassroots. Coupled with other reasons, it resulted in a slump in agricultural production for three successive years (1959–61).

Among the "other reasons" was the insanity of the "Great Leap Forward." It is impossible to believe that in the history of all humanity there has ever been a policy decision that caused more hardship and suffering than Mao's mad effort to transform the Chinese economy and society in a few brief years.

**The Great Famine, 1958–1961.** In the first blush of enthusiasm in their formation, most communes organized communal dining in which food was made available to all without cost. The Communist party encouraged communal dining to, among other things, reduce the role and influence of the family, promote economies of scale in food preparation, release most of the women for full-time farm work, and make it possible to collect household cooking utensils for use in the backyard furnaces to make iron that had no value. In 1983, in one of the most memorable moments that I have experienced in China, I asked a young man what he had thought of communal dining—he was probably eight years old when in late 1958 or early 1959 communal dining began in his village. He responded that he liked it very much, the food was good, and plentiful, and he was able to eat with his friends. After commenting on his favorable memories, he stopped for a moment before blurting out bitterly: "And then we starved." This was the beginning of what was the worst famine in the history of the world as measured by the number of deaths: a minimum of 20 million and perhaps as many as 30 million (Ashton 1984, 619). In his village, as in thousands of others, food was supplied on a lavish scale by Chinese standards during the first half year after what was claimed to be a bumper harvest in 1958; it was, however, only a good harvest. Without a price system to guide them since the food was considered to be free, the Chinese simply almost exhausted the year's supply of food well before the new harvest was available. Thus, famine occurred, not after a poor crop year but after a good harvest. The birthrate in 1958 was 15 percent below that of the year before, and the death rate increased by 11 percent (SYOC 1986, 72).

The self-delusion that affected Mao and his associates concerning what the Great Leap Forward was accomplishing in agriculture is well described by Kenneth R. Walker in his exhaustive analysis of grain supplies and procurements in the 1950s and early 1960s. Acting under the assumption that if the people willed it, it would happen, the government accepted outrageous estimates of the 1958 grain crop. The State Statistical Bureau first estimated the 1958 grain crop to be 375 million tons, but in December 1958 it reduced the estimate to 360 million tons because much of the increase had been in potatoes (potatoes are included in Chinese grain statistics on the basis of a fourth or a fifth of actual weight). As late as August 1959 Zhou Enlai put the grain production estimate at 250 million tons (Walker 1984, 138–39). This lower estimate was still far above what is now a generally agreed-upon figure of 200 million tons (SYOC 1984, 145).

In August 1958, after stating some outrageously high production figures, Mao reportedly asked listeners in a county in Hopei Province, "How can you eat your way through so much grain? What are you going to do with the surplus?" When he was told that they would exchange the surplus for machinery, Mao responded: "But what will happen if you are not the only ones to have grain surpluses and if every county has them? You may want to exchange your grain for machinery but no one will want it" (Walker 1984, 140). On the assumption that the 1958 grain crop was a bumper one, Mao initiated a policy of reducing the area used for grain production to a third of arable land.

This extraordinary proposal was made even though grain production at the time (and since) occupies about four-fifths of China's cropland. Because the great man made such a proposal, it was not surprising that the farmers reacted by cutting the grain area by almost 10 percent in 1959. The 1959 grain harvest was 35 million tons or 17.5 percent below that of 1958, and more than half of the decline stemmed from the decrease in production area induced by a thoughtless and irresponsible statement (SYOC 1984, 137). How many lives did Mao's ignorance cost? An additional 10 million tons of grain would have provided an additional 800 calories per day for two years for more than 100 million people and would have saved millions of lives.

In their lengthy history of the period, Liu Suinian and Wu Qungan (1986) discussed the establishment of the communal kitchens or canteens and the provision of free food. As of the end of 1959, they reported, it was claimed that 72 percent of the rural population took their meals in the canteens (Liu and Wu 1986, 263). And, even though there was famine during the period, the Party Central Committee issued a directive in March 1960 to continue the establishment of the canteens to serve 80–90 percent of the population.

While never mentioning that an actual famine occurred during 1958–1961—such mention apparently remains taboo today—Liu and Wu described the circumstances that brought on famine in 1958: an inappropriate policy (free food), self-delusion (unachievable grain output goals), and callous mismanagement of forced grain deliveries. According to Liu and Wu (1986, 244):

> Overestimation of the per-hectare yield of crops at that time inevitably led to an increase in the amount of grain to be delivered to the state. In 1958 the delivery of grain (agricultural tax in kind) by the farmers and the state's purchases of surplus grain increased by 22.3 percent over the year before while actual grain output increased by only 2.5 percent. The amount of grain delivered by the farmers . . . rose from 24.6 percent of the actual output of 1957 to 29.4 percent in 1958. At the same time, the practice of providing food free of charge by the public canteens had almost depleted the villages of grain. To increase the amount of grain to be delivered to the state in these circumstances, coupled with the state banks forcing farmers to pay back loans extended to them, no matter whether these loans were due or not, greatly affected the livelihood of the farmers.

The final sentence seems a very mild way of describing a series of policy mistakes and misjudgments that over a period of three years caused the deaths of millions of rural people.

In some studies of this period, it is implied that the decline in food production that occurred between 1958 and 1961—such as the decrease in grain production of 28 percent or 56 million tons—was caused by bad weather conditions. Liu and Wu (1986), however, noted that adverse climatic conditions decreased grain production by about 10–15 million tons in 1959 and 15–20 million tons in 1960 and then concluded: "But this accounted for only one-third of the total amount of decrease in grain production" (266). Of the total decline in grain production for 1959–1961, at most a fourth of it can be attributed to adverse weather. The major reason for the rest of the decline was "essentially the implementation of 'Left' policies" (266).

It is impossible to imagine stronger evidence of the urban bias of the policies of the Communist party than what occurred in rural and urban food grain consumption between 1957 and 1960. During those years, the average annual per capita food grain consumption fell 19.4 percent for the entire nation. In the cities the decline was small—only 1.7 percent—but in the countryside it was 23.7 percent (Liu and Wu 1986, 270). The 70 percent decline in pork consumption was shared equally between the city and country. In effect, starvation was imposed on the rural people to feed the urban population. There was no attempt to share the decline in food availability with the urban population. The decline in pork consumption, while large in percentage terms, had little effect on calorie intake, since the loss in consumption involved fewer than forty calories a day, which could have been absorbed by the urban population with its much higher per capita calorie intake than the rural population's.

**Industry and the Great Leap Forward.** The development of industry during the Great Leap Forward was affected by policies as irrational as those that afflicted rural people. Great emphasis was put on investment and the rapid development of heavy industry. In 1957 light industry accounted for 55 percent of industrial output; by 1960 this percentage had declined to 33 percent. Thus, much of the growth in industrial output stemmed from investment in heavy industry, from which consumers benefited relatively little. Although national income from industry more than doubled from 1957 to 1960—in part from the neglect of agriculture and the transfer of labor to the cities—most of that income gain was lost by 1962. The rupture of relations with the Soviet Union in mid-1960, which resulted in the abrupt withdrawal of thousands of engineers and technicians, had an adverse effect of unknown magnitude. The output of heavy industry, in which much of the Soviet effort was concentrated, fell by more than half from 1960 to 1962 (SYOC 1986, 32, 34).

One feature of the Great Leap Forward was that the rate of accumulation as a percentage of national income rose to unprecedented levels. Under the First Five-Year Plan the annual rate of accumulation reached a relatively high 24 percent; the planned rate for the Second Five-Year Plan was 25 percent. But with the irrational aspects of the Great Leap, the rate approached 40 percent (Xue 1986, 156). Such high rates of accumulation for an economy with a low level of income implies little interest in the material welfare of the current population.

**Recovery, 1963–1965.** Following the madness and irresponsibility of the Great Leap period, there was a gradual return to what might be called normalcy. The canteens were closed down in 1961, and the agricultural tax and state purchases of grain were reduced substantially in both 1961 and 1962, but admittedly too late to save millions from starvation. The food supply situation remained very serious through 1962. Some of the most outlandish projects carried out in the Great Leap period were halted—for example, iron-making in backyard furnaces, grand water conservancy projects, and a number of construction projects. The labor released from these and similar activities by the spring of 1961 increased the farm labor force by 29 million or by almost 15 percent compared with the year before (Liu and Wu 1986, 275). Some of the increase in the agricultural labor force resulted from sending back to the country millions of workers who had moved to the cities during the frenzy of the Great Leap. In May 1961 the Party Central Committee decided that the urban population of 130 million should be reduced by 20 million, with half to occur in 1961. A year later the goal for reduction was increased, and by mid-1963 the urban population was reduced by 26.3 million (Liu and Wu 1986, 290–292).

By no stretch of the imagination was this enormous migration a democratic one. The people who left the city had no choice about either whether they left or where they went. Nor were the ones who were forced to leave only those who had come to the cities during the Great Leap. A case in point is a man I met in 1985 who was living in a hostel for the elderly in a rural village. During the 1930s he had moved to Shanghai, where he worked as an auto mechanic. After World War II he worked for the U.S. Army in their motor pool. After they left, he was once again employed as a mechanic and remained in that job throughout the 1950s. In the campaign in the early 1960s to reduce the population of Shanghai, it was discovered that this man had come from a village. Even though he had lived in the city for nearly three decades and had no immediate family left in the village, he was forced to return to the village. Thus, in 1985 he was living in the hostel for the elderly because he had no relatives in the village. It is surprising how little attention Western scholars have paid to what must have been the largest forced migration and relocation of population that the world has ever known.

The 1958 centralization of authority over production and distribution in the communes was judged a failure by 1961. In 1962 it was decided that each commune's production team, which consisted of twenty to thirty households, should be the basic accounting unit. In this role, the production team exercised control over both production and distribution, whereas formerly control over distribution was at a higher level. It was also declared that the land, animals, and farm tools designated for use by a production team should not be changed again and that such items were then owned by the team. It was stated as well that these arrangements should remain unchanged for at least thirty years (Liu and Wu 1986, 296–97). As with almost every commitment made to rural people, however, significant parts of these commitments were violated within a decade.

During this period of recovery, there was experimentation with various production responsibility systems, similar in most respects to the systems introduced in the 1980s. In a number of areas, output quotas were fixed for individual households, and remuneration was linked to output. Responsibility plots or private plots were approved, although it remained clear that the means of production was social property.

According to Liu and Wu (1986), these efforts to rehabilitate agriculture from the harm generated by the creation of communes and the Great Leap were widely criticized. The steps were labeled as "stirring up the evil wind of going it alone" and "taking the capitalist road" (Liu and Wu 1986, 310). The provision for private plots, the extension of free markets, the establishment of small firms with responsibility for their own profits, and the institution of the responsibility system were all criticized within the Communist party as revisionist measures. Rural trade fairs, where peasants and itinerant peddlers sold their wares, were soon subjected to restrictions designed to limit their similarities to any capitalist institution of the same kind.

It was not until 1964 that the national income or the combined gross agricultural and industrial output reached the 1958 level. Thus, six years of growth had been lost. The per capita production of grain—the source of at least 85 percent of total calorie consumption in the 1960s and 1970s—did not reach the 1956–1958 level until the late 1970s.

**The Cultural Revolution, 1966–1976.** The period of some economic rationality and adjustment came to a screeching halt, however, with the launching of the Cultural Revolution in 1966 and what many Chinese now call the "Ten Years of Turmoil." According to one description of the decade, "The 'cultural revolution,' initiated by a leader labouring under a misapprehension and capitalized on by counter-revolutionary cliques, led to domestic turmoil and brought catastrophe to the Party, the state and the whole people" (Liu and Wu 1986, 340).

In mid-1966 a struggle occurred within the Communist party which must have been quite similar to that of May and June 1989. In a series of meetings in 1966, the conditions were laid for the creation of the Red Guards and the beginning of several years of turmoil and disruption. One similarity between the two periods was that eventually Chairman Mao used the People's Liberation Army to regain control of the country and to put down and disband the Red Guards by any means, including deadly force. In June 1989 Deng Xiaoping arrived at the same decision that Mao had made years before: use military force. One difference was that Deng was one of the victims of the power struggle in 1966. He was brought back by Mao in 1974, only to lose again in 1976; he reemerged a year later as vice chairman of the Communist party.

The developments and power struggles of the Cultural Revolution are described in a variety of sources, including the official statement—at least official as of the time of its writing (1981)—"On Questions of Party History." This statement dealt with more than the Cultural Revolution; it also attempted to evaluate Mao's role in the Communist party and his contributions and deficiencies. It seems safe to assume that this document represents what best served the interests of Deng Xiaoping, at least as he saw them at the time.[1]

**1976–1978.** After Mao's death in 1976, China entered a brief period that was somewhat similar to that of the Great Leap Forward. Efforts were made to promote specific examples on a wide scale without reference to the evidence or their potential validity. One such effort that had serious implications for agriculture was the movement to learn from

Dazhai, a small village in a mountainous area of China that had reported miraculous increases in farm production after literally moving mountains to create cropland. Because Mao had long held that communes everywhere should learn from Dazhai, this example continued to receive enthusiastic support from Hua Guofeng (Mao's successor as chairman of the Communist party), who presumably gave that support because of his adherence to the "two whatevers."[2] Presumably, Dazhai had carried out the great feats of constructing productive agricultural land out of mountains and barren soil solely by the use of its own labor and resources, but later it became known that much of what had been claimed for Dazhai was false. The army had assisted with the construction work, and the state had provided financial resources. In addition, it was learned that the output data had been falsified to some degree, with the degree of falsification increasing as attention on Dazhai increased.

During these years several of the measures taken by the government to remove the deleterious effects of the Cultural Revolution on agriculture, especially after 1974, were negated, and some new restrictions were imposed. More specifically, campaigns were undertaken to restrict or discourage the retention of the private plots, family sideline production, and trade fairs on the grounds that such activities represented a capitalist trend. These efforts were similar to other campaigns to cut the tail off the capitalist dog. In an evaluation of this period, Liang Wensen (1982, 61–62) observed that

> after the overthrow of the "Gang of Four" in October 1976, we once again tried to speed up development by setting targets that were much too high. This was particularly true of the impetuous and unrealistic plans put forward in 1978 which, in many ways, resembled those of 1958. Proposals were made to produce 400 million tons of grain; 60 million tons of steel; 250 million tons of oil . . . ; and to import large amounts of modern equipment and technology by the end of the Sixth Five-Year Plan (1981–1985). This clearly went beyond the real resources of the country. If 1958 can be characterized as a year of excessive haste based on "indigenous" methods, then 1978 was one of haste based on "imported" methods.

Much to the surprise of most people, China reached its goal of producing 400 million tons of grain—but in 1984. Had the agricultural policies introduced in 1978 by Hua Guofeng not been changed radically in 1979, however, the grain goal would have suffered the same fate as the steel and oil goals—substantial underfulfillment.

CHAPTER 2

# The Chinese Economy in 1978

The reforms undertaken under the leadership of Deng Xiaoping are generally attributed to decisions made at the Third Plenary Session of the Eleventh Party Central Committee held in December 1978. But as of 1978 or any later time a clear blueprint for the actual reforms undertaken apparently did not exist. They evolved over time. Nor did the reforms always move in a consistent direction toward well-articulated goals. Nonetheless, the reform process has been one of the most far-reaching ever undertaken by any economy. As of June 1989 much remained undone, however, and it is not obvious what the near future will bring. Nevertheless, it is worthwhile to try to understand the major features of the reforms and what was achieved.

This chapter will indicate briefly some of the important developments that occurred during the quarter century preceding the reform efforts initiated in 1979. The achievements of the industrial sector will be slighted, however. They were obviously purchased at great cost because of the high percentage of national output denied to a very poor population for its consumption needs and used instead for accumulation or investment, primarily in heavy industry.

## Population and Labor Force

In 1952 the population of China was 575 million, increasing to 963 million in 1978 at an annual rate of growth of 2 percent. Also in 1952, 88 percent of the population lived in rural areas, modestly decreasing to 82 percent in 1978 (SYOC 1984, 82). The modest increase in urban population stemmed, at least in part, from a policy of restricting migration into the larger cities.

The total labor force increased from 185.6 million in 1952 to 344.4 million in 1978 at an annual growth rate of 2.4 percent (or at a rate higher than the population growth rate). According to the official data, the labor force participation rate increased very little in rural areas between 1952 and 1978—only from 36.2 percent to 38.8 percent. There was a large increase in the participation rate in urban areas, however—from 34.7 percent to 55.2 percent (SYOC 1984, 81 and 107)—caused primarily by the increased participation of women in the paid labor force. As will be noted, almost all of the increase in real per capita incomes in urban areas resulted from the increase in labor force participation and not from an increase in real wage rates.

As of 1978 China remained primarily an agricultural economy, if the percentage of the labor force engaged in agriculture is used as the criterion. In that year 70.7 percent of the labor force was engaged in agriculture, down from 83.5 percent in 1952 (SYOC 1988, 127).

Agriculture's share of national income in China—68.4 percent in 1952 and 35.4 percent in 1978 (SYOC 1984, 31)—has been substantially less than its share of the labor force, but this is the situation in all developing countries and in most industrial countries. The lower share of national income (which includes only the income derived from material production)[3] than of the labor force stems from several factors, including some related to statistical convention such as valuing home-produced and home-consumed farm products at their sale price rather than at their retail value. As a result, the income created in the farm household from the processing of farm products (processing done before sale in retail markets) is ignored. The difference in shares also reflects the substantially lower real incomes of farm than nonfarm people.

## Income and Consumption

National income, in constant prices, grew at an annual rate of 6 percent from 1952 to 1978, according to the official data (SYOC 1984, 30), implying that the national income in 1978 was 4.5 times that in 1952. With population growth of 67 percent over the same period, the real national income per capita in 1978 must have been 2.7 times what it was in 1952, with an annual growth rate of 3.9 percent.

Gregory Chow (1985), however, showed that the official index of national income at comparable or constant prices significantly overstated the real growth by using agricultural and industrial product prices from 1952, when the prices of industrial products were very high relative to agricultural products. If the prices of a recent year are used for weighting agricultural and industrial products, a very different result is obtained. Chow, using 1980 price weights for agriculture and industry rather than the 1952 price weights, estimated an annual growth rate for national income of 3.9 percent for 1952–1978 (Chow 1985, 201). The annual growth rate for per capita income would then be 1.7 percent. This is a very respectable growth rate but much below what was claimed officially.

The data on real wages give a quite different impression of the probable change in the standard of living in urban areas between 1952 and 1978. In 1978 the real wages of staff and workers in state-owned units were only 15 percent greater than in 1952 and actually 11 percent less than the 1957 real wage (SYOC 1988, 160). According to an index of personal consumption for peasants and nonagricultural residents published by the State Statistical Bureau, the per capita consumption of nonagricultural residents (about the same as the households of staff and workers) increased 98 percent from 1952 to 1978 and 57 percent from 1957 to 1978 (SYOC 1988, 711). How can these changes be consistent with either a small increase or a decline in real wages? Earlier it was noted that there was a large increase in the percentage of the urban population in the labor force between 1957 and 1978. It was this increase, which was reflected in a near doubling of the number of workers per family from 1.33 to 2.38 over the same period, that made possible the greater increase in consumption than in wages. Since the average household size also fell slightly, the number of people supported by each employee, including the employee, declined from 3.29 to 1.71. Much of the increase in the number of employees per household stemmed from the increase in female participation in the labor force. Although these women had not been idle before—rather, they had been performing useful functions in the household—their functions had not been included in the national income. Thus, the growth of real income was overestimated (as is true in most economies at similar levels of income), but, given the imperfections in national income accounting, the very modest increase in real wages was consistent with the growth of consumption in view of the increase in labor force participation rates in urban areas.

Considerable skepticism, however, is warranted with respect to the estimates of increased per capita consumption between 1952 and 1978. As is generally true for complex data series, the State Statistical Bureau provides no information about how the series were constructed, and serious questions can be raised about the validity of the series on per capita consumption prior to 1978. One of the most pervasive empirical economic relationships is that as per capita real incomes increase, the percentage of income spent on food declines. This did not happen in China for either the urban or rural population. In 1957 urban staff and worker households spent 58.4 percent of their incomes on food, 59.2 percent in 1964, and 56.7 percent in 1981. Between 1957 and 1981 the per capita consumption of nonagricultural residents was estimated officially to have increased by 91 percent (SYOC 1988, 711). Peasants spent 65.8 percent of their total expenditures on food in 1957 and 67.7 percent in 1978 for a small increase (SYOC 1984, 473). The per capita consumption of peasants was supposed to have increased by 35 percent over that period.

If the increases in real consumption or real income had been as large as implied by the official estimates, there should have been a decline in the percentage of consumption expenditures devoted to food. The relationships between increases in consumption expenditures and the share of income spent on food imply income elasticities of demand for food of 1 or perhaps even more. Even at the low income levels found in China during the 1960s and 1970s, the income elasticity of demand for food was significantly less than unity according to estimates made by Hendrik Houthakker (Chow 1985, 167). Houthakker, using data for 1930, estimated that the expenditure elasticity of demand for food was 0.62 in Shanghai and 0.59 in Beijing.

Assuming that the elasticity of food expenditures to total consumption expenditures was 0.7 during the 1950s (significantly higher than Houthakker's estimates for 1930), one can estimate how much the percentage of total consumer expenditures allocated to food should have declined if real per capita consumption levels had increased either 50 or 100 percent. The 50 percent increase is used as an approximation for the reported increase in real consumption by peasants, while the latter approximates the claimed increase for staff and workers between 1952 and 1978 or 1957 and 1981. If then one assumes that the percentage of total expenditures devoted to food was 60 percent in 1952, an increase in real consumption of 50 percent would have meant that food's share should have decreased to 54 percent. If real consumption had increased by 100 percent, food's share of total expenditures should have declined to 51 percent. Instead, as indicated above, the expenditures of urban staff and worker households on food as a share of total expenditures decreased from 58.4 percent in 1957 to 56.7 percent in 1981. Data are not available for 1978, but since there was a significant increase in incomes of urban families between 1978 and 1981, the percentage of consumer expenditures devoted to food in 1978 could have been at the same level as in 1957. The data indicate, however, that peasants increased the share of their consumer expenditures devoted to food between 1957 and 1978.

Estimates of housing space per capita for peasants for 1957 and 1978 indicate a decline from 11.3 square meters in 1957 to 10.2 square meters in 1978 (SYOC 1986, 582)—housing space includes space devoted to production purposes as well as to living quarters. Living space in urban areas declined even more than in the rural areas. In 182 large and medium-sized cities in 1952 the urban living space was 4.5 square meters; by 1978 it had declined 20 percent to 3.6 square meters (Taubman 1985, 183). In all urban areas in 1978 living space per capita was 4.2 square meters or 44 square feet (SYOC 1984, 453).

Xue, the elder statesman among Chinese economists, was much closer to the mark than the State Statistical Bureau when he wrote: "Between 1957 and 1977, living standards almost remained the same. The average wage was not raised, the peasants' food grain was not increased, and about one in every three peasants led a hard life" (Xue 1981, 176).

Xue was correct in noting that the peasants' food grain had not increased. Data for the entire population reveal that in 1957 the per capita consumption of food grains was 203 kilograms; in 1978 consumption was 195 kilograms. Other evidence points out that the per capita consumption of grain of urban dwellers did not decline relative to that of farm residents.

Nor is there any evidence that there were increases in other foods to offset the decline in per capita consumption of grain in any measurable degree. The State Statistical Bureau estimated that per capita calorie consumption was 2,270 in 1952 and 2,311 in 1978. Because grain consumption was somewhat higher in 1957 than in 1952, per capita calorie consumption in 1957 and 1978 should have been approximately the same. Between 1952 and 1978 the calorie availability from animal products increased from 111 to 142 per day. Vegetable products provided 95 percent of total calories in 1957 and 94 percent in 1978 (SYOC 1984, 480). Grain accounted for 88 percent of all calories in 1952 and 87 percent in 1978, essentially no change (Piazza 1986, 83–84).

One area of consumption in which peasants had better conditions than urban dwellers was housing. In 1978 peasants had 8.1 square meters of *living* space per capita—almost double that of urban residents. One important difference between rural and urban residents is that peasants must pay the full costs of their housing—its construction, maintenance, and heating—while urban residents receive their housing nearly free of charge. In 1981 urban residents allocated only 1.4 percent of their total expenditures for rent and 1 percent for water and electricity, for a total of 2.4 percent for rent and utilities. Peasants, in contrast, allocated 10 percent of their expenditures to housing costs and 5.7 percent for fuel and utilities for a total of 15.7 percent (SYOC 1988, 717 and 734).

Urban housing deteriorated in both quantity and quality over the quarter century. The urban population grew rapidly and the housing stock failed to keep pace. In 1978, as noted earlier, the average amount of floor space in all urban areas was 4.2 square meters (44 sq. ft.). This is an area a little larger than 6 x 7 feet. In Shanghai the urban living space was not much more than 3 square meters, which is little more than the area of a standard double bed.

## Inequality

One striking claim made by Chinese officials—and echoed by many Western visitors to China from 1960 to 1977—was that while per capita income and consumption growth had been modest in China, the inequality of income distribution had been greatly reduced. A related claim was that famine had been conquered. When on each point China was compared to India, India was cast in an unfavorable light. After all, in India poor people, including the homeless, were everywhere, but in China's cities tourists did not see beggars or the very poor. Thus the surface indications seemed consistent with the claims.

There were in fact substantial reductions in income inequality in urban areas and within rural production teams, but it is now clear that the egalitarian emphasis explained a significant part of the poor performance of the Chinese economy. The egalitarian outcome was achieved through breaking the connection between productivity and reward—between the outcome of work and pay. Egalitarianism was represented by the notion of "everyone eating out of the same big pot," regardless of how much or little the person contributed to what was in the big pot. Thus, in both agriculture and industry there was little incentive to work hard or effectively or, in some cases, at all. By following such principles, urban workers, as well as members of a given production team or production brigade (where the brigade was the accounting unit) achieved a high degree of income equality.

Xue Muqiao noted that in a socialist economy the distribution of goods among individuals should be based upon the adage "to each according to his work." He also noted the serious adverse effects of the emphasis upon egalitarianism that characterized the Cultural Revolution:

> For at least a decade, the system based upon "to each according to his work" was seriously undermined, causing tremendous losses to industrial and agricultural production and preventing improvement in the people's livelihood. Major efforts will have to be made in the forthcoming years to rehabilitate, consolidate and perfect such a system of distribution. The fallacious notions spread by Lin Biao and the Gang of Four to distort and discredit this system should be thoroughly criticized and its tremendous impetus to the development of productive forces fully explained (Xue 1981, 77–78)

Xue failed to mention the many contributions Mao made to egalitarianism, including his haste to create communes, his support of "learning from Dazhai," and his agreeing to limits placed on private plots, sideline activities, and industrial activities in rural areas.

The practice of allocating income within production teams, generally on the basis of time worked with little or no regard to the quality of work, resulted in a relatively egalitarian distribution within each team. The major factor creating differences in family incomes within the same team was labor power—number of workers—and during the Cultural Revolution some communes distributed grain on a per capita basis to assist families with more dependents per worker. According to Griffin and Griffin (1985), however, data obtained from several production teams do not support the presumption of income equality within teams. Their investigations showed a considerable degree of variability in per capita household incomes.

But however equally incomes may have been distributed within production teams, there were great inequalities among production teams even within the same village. Determination of the amount and quality of land assigned to production teams was apparently quite haphazard, and there was no systematic mechanism for changing land allocations among teams as time went on. Moreover, differences in income stemming from differences in quality of management could not be corrected by migration from one team to another, either within a village or from one village to another.

On the changes in income inequality in rural China under the communes, Xue Muqiao concluded:

> The differences in living standards among peasants are even more pronounced than those among the workers or between workers and peasants. In the more than two decades since the completion of the movement to set up agricultural producers' cooperatives, differences between communes, brigades and teams have not narrowed but have continued to widen (Xue 1981, 101).

Earlier in the same work Xue (1981, 99) had noted that there had been no narrowing, but possibly a widening, of differences in living standards between workers and peasants, indicating that nationally the difference has been about 2 to 1 but that "it exceeds 2 to 1 in most areas and is as high as 3 or 4 to 1 in some areas."

Some data on Wugong, a village in Hebei Province, indicate the degree of income inequality that existed within what might appear to the casual observer to be a relatively homogeneous community with modest differences in the quality of its land. The village had a population of about 2,500 in the late 1970s and three production teams. From 1972 to 1979 an average per capita income of 142 yuan was distributed to Team 1, 118 yuan to Team 2, and 192 yuan to Team 3, for a difference of more than 60 percent between the highest and lowest incomes. The Wugong brigade belonged in the Wugong commune. In 1974 a per capita income of 80 yuan was distributed to the commune, compared to 191 yuan to Team 3 and 165 yuan to the brigade. For three years in the 1970s the lowest-income brigade in the commune had a distributed income of 40 yuan compared with 195 yuan for Team 3 (Selden 1980). This is an income ratio of nearly 5:1, which solidly contradicts the view that inequality had been eliminated in rural areas. It is quite probable that under the communes inequality increased because some market mechanisms that had previously prevailed and contributed to reduced inequality had been eliminated.

Data on net income per capita for 20 of the 29 provinces for 1978 reveal wide differences in peasant incomes. Hebei Province had the lowest per capita peasant income of 92 yuan, though other provinces—such as Gansu, Guizhou, Anhui, and Sichuan—were considered to be poorer than Hebei. These four low-income provinces had per capita incomes ranging from 98 to 117 yuan and a rural population of 151 million (SYOC 1986, 73 and 586). Jiangsu Province had the highest per capita income of 290 yuan and Beijing was second with 225 yuan. The national average in 1978 was 134 yuan. In 1980, after substantial price increases but before the adoption of the responsibility system, Shanghai had the highest per capita rural income at 397 yuan, and Shaanxi had the lowest at 142 yuan.

## Hunger and Famine

The evidence is clear that the hunger and famine stemming from the enormous famine of 1958–1961 were not eliminated. As many as 30 million people died then, primarily because of inept policies, including the greater weight that Mao gave to national self-reliance than to the avoidance of human suffering. Maintaining independence from the international community may or may not be a meritorious policy if associated with appropriate domestic measures, but in no case can the deaths of millions be justified by emphasis upon such a political ideal. Sufficient grain was available from the major exporting countries to have met the production shortfalls in China from 1959 to 1961 (Johnson 1990).

A Central Committee document of December 1978 stated that 100 million peasants had insufficient grain. Reportedly in Anhui Province "there are many people in the villages who have not enough to eat or enough clothing to keep them warm." The *People's Daily* (May 14, 1980) stated that "in some parts of the country containing in all 100 million people, there has never been a good life since the collectivization and production has not picked up since the three years of economic collapse. In these regions the population has increased but the amount of grain has not increased. . . . The peasants have lost their faith in collectivization." And well they should have.

**But Significant Improvements**

Although the commune system had many shortcomings and failures, the picture of life in the countryside in the late 1970s should not be painted too bleakly. While it is true that the real incomes of peasants increased by only a few percent between 1957 and 1977 and urban incomes increased at a modest rate, there is evidence of substantial improvements in the living conditions of the Chinese people, including those living in rural areas. A major part of the evidence is found in the sharp increase in life expectancy, including a substantial decline in infant mortality, and increased literacy. Life expectancy at birth was thirty-six years for 1950, increasing to sixty-four years for 1979 (World Bank 1983, 98).

Data on life expectancy in urban areas during the 1950s indicate that the urban bias is nothing new in China. In 1950 life expectancy in Beijing was 54 years for males and 50 years for females, increasing to 61 and 60 years, respectively, in 1953. In 1957 life expectancy at birth was 57 years in 70 cities and 126 towns (SYOC 1984, 95). For the same periods, infant mortality declined from 236 deaths per thousand births to 65 deaths per thousand. Twenty-seven percent of children were in elementary school in 1950, increasing to 67 percent in 1960 and to 90 percent in 1980. Secondary school enrollment was about 20 percent of the relevant age group in 1960, increasing to 40 percent in 1980 (World Bank 1983).

## CHAPTER 3

# Agricultural and Rural Policy Reforms

Any discussion of rural reforms and some of their important effects will benefit from a brief description of how agriculture was structured in China in 1978, the year that the first steps of policy reforms were formulated. As will become clear, policy reforms did not come forth in full bloom. In several important respects, subsequent events determined the particular measures that were approved.

In 1978, 294 million people were employed in agriculture out of a total of 303 million collective and individual laborers in rural areas (SYOC 1984, 107 and 109). The national labor force that year was 398.6 million. People employed in agriculture were organized into 52,780 communes, each of which had an average of thirteen brigades, which in turn were made up of seven to ten production teams. The total population of the communes was a little more than 800 million, averaging about 15,000 per commune. Each production team averaged about thirty-five households and sixty workers. A commune was the approximate size of a township in the American Midwest or thirty-six square miles.

The commune was both a political (governmental) and economic organization. It fulfilled most local government functions, including police, justice, welfare, and education, and provided family planning and medical services. The commune also had a monopoly on economic functions—assignment of production plans to the brigades and production teams, allocation of procurement quotas imposed by the state, and control over the leadership of the brigades and production teams. The commune, including all of its units, also determined how incomes were allocated to individual workers and how much was in cash or in kind and who was assigned to specific jobs, even on a daily basis. Given the numerous restrictions that evolved during the Cultural Revolution on most forms of private activities—restrictions on the size and use of private plots, handicraft production, and other private sideline activities plus the many restrictions on rural fairs and markets—the collective organizations had enormous power over the lives of rural people. Mao also envisaged communes with military functions, though the reason for these is questionable other than to supply most of the recruits for the People's Liberation Army.

The relatively low level of economic development of the communes was indicated by the share of incomes paid in money. Xue estimated that the collectives distributed about one-fourth of their incomes in money and the rest in kind (Xue 1981, 97). An important implication of such a proportion was that annual incomes were closely related to the annual output of farm products, especially grain, of each production team.

## Summary of Policy Reforms

The reforms agreed upon in December 1978 in the now famous communiqué of the Third Plenary Session of the Eleventh Central Committee of the Communist Party of China and implemented in 1979 were wide-ranging in nature and revealed starkly the extent of interventions in the lives of farm people that had been carried out in response to the mindless acceptance of ill-founded ideological views. These changes represented only first steps, however; the more sweeping changes such as the introduction of responsibility systems and the abolition of the communes did not come until later—eighteen months later for the responsibility systems and at least four years for the communes.

The major reforms announced in late 1978 or in 1979 were (Economic Research Service 1980, 3–5):

- substantial increases in the purchase prices of eighteen farm products: 20 percent for grains, 25 percent for fats and oils, 15 percent for cotton, 26 percent for pigs, and 20–50 percent for the other fourteen products. (Bonuses for deliveries in excess of procurement quotas were provided for grain, 50 percent; fats and oils, 25 percent; and cotton, 30 percent.)
- increases in agricultural investment from 10.7 percent of total state investment in 1978 to 14 percent in 1979
- reinstitution of the Chinese Agricultural Bank
- reaffirmation of three-level ownership by the commune, brigade, and production team, with the production team acting as the basic unit for production, management, and distribution
- approval of specialization of agricultural production according to local conditions. (This measure repudiated Mao's policy of regional self-sufficiency in grain production.)
- incentives for cotton production, including fixed grain procurement quotas and guarantees of grain rations; production contracts between provinces and production teams; increased supplies of farm inputs; and a further increase in procurement prices announced at the end of 1979
- expression of support for the activation of village trade fairs
- clarification of the role and legality of private production, including private plots, in the constitution
- reduction in rural taxes, including taxes on commune enterprises, reducing the rural tax to 3.35 percent of total output value, and exempting low-yield and grain-deficit areas from agricultural taxes
- reduction in the percentage of surplus grains (from 90 to 70) required for sale to the state
- emphasis on control of population growth as an important condition for the success of the "Four Modernizations."

These changes were followed by others. Without regard to the timing, later important policy modifications permitted farmers to sell directly to the urban population, established wholesale markets in urban areas for farm products, permitted farmers to become marketing agents with the right to buy from others and to resell without being accused of realizing unearned income, and made it possible for private individuals to engage in transportation activities both for themselves and for hire.

Some changes occurred with breathtaking speed; others seemed to require more time than one might have anticipated given other changes that occurred. An example is the halting way in which the restrictions that had long affected the sale of farm products by rural people were lifted or changed. According to an article in the *China Agriculture Yearbook* (1987, 49):

> For a long time, Chinese farmers were barred from the market, because the system of mandatory purchase of farm products was carried out by the State. After the . . . [December 1978 session] of the Communist Party, rural fairs were allowed to resume activities and farmers began to enter the field of market exchange. But they could only sell some products on the nearby rural fairs which the State did not purchase. In 1983 the State began to narrow the scope of the products for mandatory purchase, allow more products to go to the markets and allow farmers to engage in long distance transport and marketing of goods. It was only after that some farmers began to quit production to take up transportation of farm products, giving rise to a large number of households specialized in long distance transport and marketing of goods or in business and handicraft. The number of such people soared after 1985 when the mandatory purchase of farm produce by the State was reformed.

Thus, a major reason for the delay in permitting farm people the freedom to market their own goods, to engage in buying and selling, and to provide transport services was to maintain the monopoly of the state procurement agency. It therefore appears that unregulated monopoly is bad for the people in both socialist and capitalist economies. Undoubtedly, the resistance of the procurement agency was reinforced by continued pressure from the ideologues, who held that any private activity represented a damaging departure from the principles of Marxism, as interpreted by the radical wing of the Chinese Communists.

## Two Major Changes

Designation of the emergence of the household responsibility system and the abolition of the commune as two major organizational and institutional changes does not imply that the many other changes were unimportant. Certainly the effects of the household responsibility system would have been much more modest had the other changes not occurred.

**Emergence of the household responsibility system.** The household responsibility system emerged as the predominant system out of a dozen or more different types. Under this system, land is assigned to a family. The family is then responsible for meeting the procurement goals assigned to it and making payments to the village to cover certain costs such as welfare and maintenance of joint facilities. After meeting these obligations, the family has full control over the net income realized.

At its institution the responsibility system was not entirely new, since it had been used in some areas during the recovery period after the Great Leap Forward. It had a short trial, however, because of the onset of the Cultural Revolution. In 1979 the household responsibility system was tried out by only eighteen households in Fengyang County, Anhui Province (FBIS-CHI-88-227, Nov. 25, 1988, 45). After a one-year trial it was declared a success, and by mid-1980 the idea had received the approval of the Communist party.

During a visit I made to a farm family in Fengyang County who had participated in the trial of the system, the host, in keeping with the usual pattern encountered by foreigners, began by telling how bad things used to be. But instead of referring to how terrible conditions were before the Communists took over, as I had assumed, he was referring to the period before 1978 when he worked under the control of the commune. In the 1970s Anhui was a poor area and Fengyang County was probably reasonably representative of the province. When asked what incomes had been in the village before the changes instituted in 1979, my host replied that in 1977 each of the twenty-three households in the village sent someone to beg around the country. In his own household, which had eight members, five left the village to beg, following the standard pattern of leaving after the harvest and returning in time for the spring work. He implied that in each of several prior years he had gone out to beg so that he would not consume part of the family's limited food supply. Reportedly, in some of the poorest areas of rural China begging was officially approved and people were permitted to leave the villages to beg, but it was far more compelling to hear an individual describe his own experiences.

This farmer obviously considered the reforms a great success. Before 1978 each worker in his production team had received 0.19 yuan per day or 69 yuan per year. At the end of the year the value of the food supplied in each family's food quota was then subtracted from the total payment earned by the able-bodied workers in the family. This farmer's family, which had three workers, generally had a deficit that had to be covered with cash from a poultry sideline. In 1986, however, his family had a net income of 6,000 yuan, a far cry from the 300 yuan that they received annually in the 1970s.

The reported improvement in grain production with the introduction of the responsibility system was remarkable. In 1977 total grain production in the village was 35,000 kilograms (343 kilograms per capita). In 1979, the first year of the responsibility system, it more than doubled to 80,000 kilograms. In 1986 grain production reached 265,000 kilograms. These increases were far greater than those occurring at the national level. The low level of grain production in 1977 may mean that the communes were even less effective in this area than in the nation in motivating its members to work. Although this farmer and his village may not be typical of what happened in China generally, they do illustrate how one very poor farmer, and one small, poor village responded to the household responsibility system.

The approval of the responsibility system in mid-1980 says something—perhaps a great deal—about the decision-making process in China during the 1980s. After the household responsibility system was operated on a trial basis in Fengyang County in 1979 and was declared to be a resounding success (even though it is said to have involved only eighteen families), the results of the trial were presented to the Central Committee of the Communist party, and within a matter of a few months a policy change was made that had enormous implications for the organization of economic activities in rural China. Because Deng was a strong supporter of the responsibility system in the early 1960s, it probably did not require much evidence to convince him that the system deserved another trial.

Apparently, it was never intended, however, that the responsibility system would be universal. The first approval indicated that the system would be used only in the poorest 20 percent of the rural areas of China, and the trial in Anhui had been in such an area. A cynic might argue that the central government wanted to reduce its responsibility for meeting the minimum needs of these farm people by permitting them the freedom to farm more or less as they pleased. Because the farms in these areas were not major contributors to urban food supplies and frequently required grain to supplement their own meager production, there appeared to be little risk in giving them greater freedom.

The responsibility system spread rapidly, however, not just in the poor areas but throughout China. Although the Chinese government never publicly modified its position that the system be applied only in poor areas, apparently once the positive effects were evident, there was no stopping its spread in spite of considerable resistance from the local bureaucracies, especially the cadres in the communes. By the end of 1980, 14.4 percent of all households had adopted the system; by the end of 1981, 45.1 percent; and by the end of 1982, 80.4 percent (Lin 1986). By the end of 1983 less than 3 percent of households had not adopted the responsibility system. Thus, a radical change that involved 185 million households and nearly 800 million people occurred in approximately three years, with over half of it occurring in a period of eighteen months from July 1981 to December 1982.

**Abolition of communes.** Was it ever intended that the communes be eliminated as an institution? Probably not. It is known, however, that in the early 1980s, when the Chinese constitution was being revised, the intention was to separate the communes' governmental functions from their economic functions, thereby reducing their monopoly on power. The communes controlled almost all aspects of the lives of their members.

The intention was to transfer the governmental functions to villages and townships. In the two or three villages that I visited in the summer of 1983 the separation of functions into governmental and economic management was viewed with considerable cynicism. It was believed that the same people would carry out the same functions; only the organizational name would be changed. As shall be argued later, in some regards it was probably unfortunate that events did not work out that way. There was never an adequate plan for transferring the governmental functions actually carried out by communes to governmental units. Thus, at least in some areas, the quality of local services such as schools and medical services was adversely affected.

By the end of 1983 governments and communes were separated in 11,886 communes (SYOC 1984, 131), and by the end of 1984 the process was essentially completed; only 249 communes remained in which the government and the commune were not separated (CAY 1985, 94). At the end of 1984 there were 91,171 township governments and 926,000 village boards. In addition, there were 28,000 people's communes of economic organizations (CAY 1985, 94). The latter were the agricultural, industrial, and commercial corporations formed, generally at the township level, to take over the nonagricultural enterprise functions previously created and controlled by the communes. The enterprises formerly operated by brigades are now village industries. With these changes the communes lost their functions.

These changes in the administrative structures of rural communities clearly increased the control that the ordinary farm family had over its affairs. Adoption of the household responsibility system was perhaps more important than the abolition of the commune in increasing freedom in the countryside. Also important was the removal of almost all constraints on engaging in nonagricultural activities. A farmer who can enter the lucrative trade of transportation, as millions have, is much freer than one who is forced to devote full attention to a small plot of land and told what to grow on it besides. It is unfair, however, to leave the impression that farm people in China have anything approaching the freedom from arbitrary controls that exists in North America or Western Europe. Village and other local officials still have enormous power over the lives of farm people (see Chapter 8). While in this respect life now is much better than in the 1970s, there is still a long way to go before there are free and independent farmers in China.

### Effects of Reforms on Output

Because so many changes and reforms occurred over a short period of time, it is difficult to determine the effects of each of the most important changes on agricultural output and the real incomes of farm people. Perhaps the two most important reforms or changes of the early period from 1979 to 1984 were the introduction of the responsibility system and the increase in prices received by farmers. The price increases resulted not only from the increases in prices paid by the government but also from the greater freedom to market products at the rural fairs and markets. The increased access of farmers to urban markets did not have an important effect until near the end of the period.

From 1979 to 1984 agricultural output grew at an annual compound rate of 7.7 percent and increased by 56 percent (SYOC 1988, 35). After that, the growth rate declined to the very respectable rate of 4 percent for 1985–1988 (SYOC 1988, 35), during which the population grew at an annual rate of 1.5 percent. Thus, the recent production growth rate has exceeded the population growth rate by a substantial margin. The production growth rate from 1985 to 1988 was almost double the rate from 1956 to 1978, the period of collectivized agriculture. For that period the annual growth rate was 2.56 percent, only moderately above the population growth rate of 1.96 percent.

The rapid increase in output growth rate can be attributed to a number of factors. These include the substantial increase in prices, increased inputs, changes in the traditional forms of productivity, and institutional and organizational changes. In fact, there are more possible sources of growth than there are data or the analytical tools needed to distinguish them. One approach, however, is to estimate the effect of the increase in inputs upon the output and designate the remainder as productivity growth. This is done by comparing the change in national income with the change in inputs used in an economy over a period of time and using the residual as a measure of productivity growth. One can then proceed to determining how the growth in productivity can be partitioned between the two other important sources of growth: prices and institutional changes.

Justin Lin (1986) approached the problem by estimating a production function for agriculture using provincial data for four years (1980–1983). On the basis of this production function he was able to determine how much output in each province was due to productivity change. He then included in the analysis the rate of adoption of the household responsibility system for each province for the four years to determine how much of the productivity change was associated with changes in the system. He found that the full adoption of the household responsibility system increased resource productivity by 14 percent.

The actual extent of adoption from 1980 to 1983 was 83.5 percent, so that for these four years, adoption would have increased productivity by 12 percent. The actual increase in agricultural output was 26 percent, of which approximately 45 percent could be attributed to the shift to the household responsibility system and about 50 percent to increased inputs. For this period almost all of the increase in productivity was associated with the organizational change.

Prices did not enter directly into the estimation because the estimates were based on cross-section data. Thus, although prices may have changed from year to year, the changes were approximately the same for all provinces. What varied from province to province was the rate of adoption of the household responsibility system and changes in the quantities of inputs used. Obviously, it was not assumed that prices had no effect on agricultural output, but it was assumed that the price effect was reflected through changes in the inputs used.

The effect of the household responsibility system on productivity can be attributed to the change in incentive structure that it involved. Under the commune system there was very little relationship between the quantity and quality of labor input and the reward received. Pay was determined on the basis of the work point system, in which work points reflected the time worked and the skill required for or the difficulty of the work. Actual work points varied little from one job to another, the primary differentiation being between males and females, with females receiving only 0.8 of a work point while males received 1.0 work point. Under the responsibility system, however, the worker received the full marginal product of his or her efforts. After meeting the delivery requirements required by the state and making minimal payments to the local authorities, the rest of the output belonged to the farm family. Consequently, if additional work, in terms of either quantity or diligence in application, had a positive effect upon output, such was rewarded by the full value of its marginal product. Under the commune system, workers acted as though there was very little relationship between their contribution and their income. Thus, there was a great deal of shirking, and the quality of supervision was not sufficient to prevent it. Under the household responsibility system the shirking came to a halt—there was nothing to gain by shirking.

In an extension and refinement of his earlier work, Lin (1987a) arrived at a somewhat higher output effect—19.7 percent—from full adoption of the household responsibility system. This would account for 62 percent of the output growth during 1980–1983. Although this may seem like a high estimate, if one considers the effect of the adoption of the responsibility system upon output growth for the entire period, then Lin's higher estimate of its effect accounts for a little less than a fourth of the increased output from 1979 to 1988. That the change in institutional arrangements that occurred mostly in a brief span of time was the major source of productivity change does not seem that unreasonable. This is particularly true as the move to the household responsibility system produced disruptions in the use of machinery and the delivery and allocation of agricultural inputs.

In a second approach, John McMillan, John Whalley, and Li Jing Zu (1989) measured the effect of the household responsibility system on the change in total factor productivity from 1979 to 1983. Since their analysis was based on a time-series, it was necessary to estimate directly the effect of the price increases on productivity change, which they did by decomposing the productivity change to a price component and an incentive component. Their analysis assumed that the primary effect of the household responsibility system was to change the incentive to work and in a positive manner. They estimated that under the commune system commune members worked as if they were receiving only one-third of the value of their marginal product; thus the responsibility system accounted for 78 percent of the increase in factor productivity and 62 percent of output growth. The price increases had two effects on total output. First, they provided an incentive for labor, accounting for 22 percent of the productivity improvement or 15 percent of the output growth. Second, they induced the use of larger amounts of each input, accounting for 16 percent of the increase in output.

James Wen (1989) applied a third approach by estimating a supply function for the period 1950–1987. He regressed the level of agricultural output upon three different price variables—the general index of purchasing prices of farm products, the general index of retail prices of industrial products in rural areas, and the price index of goods and services consumed by farmers—and the percentage of households operating under the household responsibility system. The latter was taken equal to zero through 1979 and to 100 from 1984 to 1987. The estimate then derived was that full adoption of the household responsibility system was associated with an increase in productivity of 31 percent (Wen 1989, 80). Because farm production increased by 60 percent from 1979 to 1987, the adoption of the responsibility system and associated reforms accounted for 51 percent of the total increase in output. Wen's results cannot be directly compared to those of either Lin or McMillan et al., however, because a longer period of time was involved in the analysis.

TABLE 1 Indexes of Agricultural Outputs and Inputs and Two Measures of Total Factor Productivity, 1952–1988

| Year | Output index[a] | Total input index[b] | Factor productivity indexes | |
|---|---|---|---|---|
| | | | Linear | Logarithmic[c] |
| 1952 | 100.000 | 100.000 | 100.000 | 100.000 |
| 1953 | 103.099 | 103.479 | 99.6333 | 99.6567 |
| 1954 | 106.612 | 107.746 | 98.9468 | 99.0890 |
| 1955 | 114.669 | 110.491 | 103.782 | 104.037 |
| 1956 | 120.455 | 115.680 | 104.128 | 105.205 |
| 1957 | 124.793 | 121.934 | 102.345 | 103.674 |
| 1958 | 127.814 | 122.076 | 104.701 | 113.071 |
| 1959 | 110.385 | 117.104 | 94.2627 | 98.9574 |
| 1960 | 96.4417 | 123.047 | 78.3778 | 83.5611 |
| 1961 | 94.1180 | 120.735 | 77.9540 | 79.7737 |
| 1962 | 99.9277 | 124.872 | 80.0240 | 81.3473 |
| 1963 | 111.547 | 134.382 | 83.0072 | 85.5001 |
| 1964 | 126.652 | 147.387 | 85.9319 | 90.6601 |
| 1965 | 137.110 | 157.968 | 86.7959 | 93.7062 |
| 1966 | 148.962 | 174.344 | 85.4412 | 95.4311 |
| 1967 | 151.286 | 172.247 | 87.8306 | 96.3856 |
| 1968 | 147.568 | 169.187 | 87.2216 | 94.2124 |
| 1969 | 149.194 | 179.871 | 82.9450 | 91.3526 |
| 1970 | 166.391 | 202.987 | 81.9713 | 95.3526 |
| 1971 | 165.330 | 216.075 | 76.5151 | 90.7025 |
| 1972 | 163.657 | 226.722 | 72.1839 | 87.7982 |
| 1973 | 177.160 | 231.443 | 76.5455 | 93.3123 |

*(continued on next page)*

What is significant is that three very different approaches indicate that adoption of the responsibility system had a significant effect on agricultural productivity and output. Since the institutional change did not require any real resources, the output gain was, in effect, a costless increase. The savings in the real resources required to have achieved the same increase in real output under the commune system was enormous. A conservative estimate is that in terms of 1980 prices, the institutional change had an output effect equal to that obtained from an increase in inputs of 40 billion yuan or a little more than 20 percent of the gross value of agricultural output in 1980. And this increase in input cost would have been required each year—not just once. Even averaged over a billion people, 40 billion yuan represents

TABLE 1 (continued)

| Year | Output index[a] | Total input index[b] | Factor productivity indexes | |
|---|---|---|---|---|
| | | | Linear | Logarithmic[c] |
| 1974 | 183.363 | 234.963 | 78.0392 | 95.2645 |
| 1975 | 189.246 | 249.829 | 75.7500 | 95.3073 |
| 1976 | 188.364 | 248.396 | 75.8323 | 94.7672 |
| 1977 | 187.507 | 252.810 | 74.1689 | 93.5619 |
| 1978 | 202.705 | 261.208 | 77.6030 | 100.890 |
| 1979 | 218.079 | 270.876 | 80.5087 | 106.976 |
| 1980 | 229.979 | 275.831 | 83.3770 | 111.494 |
| 1981 | 243.705 | 278.869 | 87.3905 | 116.752 |
| 1982 | 271.066 | 289.446 | 93.6499 | 126.319 |
| 1983 | 292.316 | 279.612 | 104.544 | 137.088 |
| 1984 | 327.901 | 267.296 | 122.673 | 156.283 |
| 1985 | 339.316 | 262.409 | 129.308 | 162.319 |
| 1986 | 351.023 | 270.649 | 129.697 | 165.237 |
| 1987 | 371.382 | 280.132 | 132.574 | 171.436 |
| 1988 | 383.267 | 289.113 | 132.566 | 173.740 |

a. Index of gross value added. Includes some double counting of feed materials and livestock production. Excludes all sidelines except household production.
b. Index of inputs weighted by relative importance in 1952 and used to calculate the linear function of the factor productivity index.
c. Inputs converted to logarithms and weighted by relative importance in 1952.
SOURCE: James Wen. 1989. "The Current Tenure System and Its Impact on Long-Term Performance of the Farming Sector: The Case of Modern China." Ph.D. diss., Department of Economics, University of Chicago, Statistical Appendix.

annually a lot of resources and did so especially in 1980 when per capita consumption was under 230 yuan (SYOC 1988, 709).

Wen's estimate of the resources gained from the replacement of the commune system with the household responsibility system is based on the assumption that under the commune system there was no improvement in productivity from 1958 to 1978. If inputs are weighted logarithmically, total factor productivity declined from an index of 113 in 1958 to 100 in 1978 and never reached 100 in the intervening years. Consequently, the output increases achieved over the twenty years required input increases at least proportional to the gain in output.

Table 1 provides measures of agricultural outputs and inputs and two estimates of total factor productivity for 1952–1988. The data show the sharp departure from the stagnation or decline in productivity that characterized the mid-1950s until 1978. Starting in 1979 productivity increased rapidly. The data for 1979–1984 support the three analyses just summarized which found that the introduction of the household responsibility system had a major salutory effect upon productivity and thus upon agricultural output. The substantial increase in productivity in 1979 was probably associated with the effects of the output price increases and the affirmation that the production team was to be the basic unit for production, management, and distribution rather than the brigade or the commune. Productivity increased by 4.8 percent in 1981 (the first year after the significant increase in the adoption of the responsibility system), by more than 8 percent in both 1982 and 1983, and by 14 percent in 1984. In 1984 the weather was relatively good, and the large increase should be discounted by an unknown degree. The cumulated productivity increase for 1981–1984 was 39 percent.

In the years after 1984—the year the responsibility system became universal—the average rate of productivity growth declined, but to a respectable 2.6 percent. This rate is somewhat higher than the rate for U.S. agriculture for the decade ending in 1987. Thus, after the household responsibility system was adopted, the level of agricultural output in China was significantly higher than it had been before or would have been had the policies that prevailed in 1978 been maintained. Probably not all of the improvement in productivity after 1980, however, resulted from the adoption of the household responsibility system. Other changes such as the expansion of permitted activities and the sale of means of production to farm people were complementary to the responsibility system by increasing the alternative return to labor—when the value of a resource increases, special efforts are made to use that resource more productively.

### Effects of Reforms on Rural Employment

Probably no one accurately anticipated the large shift in employment in rural areas from agriculture to nonagricultural activities that followed the various policy changes that opened up economic activities formerly prohibited or drastically restricted. Table 2 presents data on the distribution of the total rural labor force among economic activities for 1970–1988. The data for 1970–1977 were estimated assuming a constant employment in agriculture of staff and workers, including

TABLE 2 Distribution of the Rural Labor Force among Economic Activities, 1970–1988 (millions)

| Year | Collective and individual laborers in rural areas (1) | Total in agriculture (2) | Staff and workers in agriculture (3) | Collective and individual laborers in agriculture[a] (4) | Nonagricultural employment of rural laborers[b] (5) |
|---|---|---|---|---|---|
| 1970 | 281.2 | 278.1 | 5.7 | 272.4 | 8.8 |
| 1971 | 287.5 | 283.4 | 6.1 | 277.3 | 10.2 |
| 1972 | 286.5 | 282.3 | 6.2 | 276.1 | 10.5 |
| 1973 | 292.6 | 288.6 | 6.5 | 282.1 | 10.5 |
| 1974 | 296.8 | 292.2 | 6.8 | 285.4 | 11.3 |
| 1975 | 299.5 | 294.6 | 7.2 | 287.4 | 12.1 |
| 1976 | 301.4 | 294.4 | 7.7 | 286.7 | 14.7 |
| 1977 | 302.5 | 293.4 | 8.2 | 285.2 | 17.3 |
| 1978 | 306.4 | 283.8 | 8.9 | 274.9 | 31.5 |
| 1979 | 310.2 | 286.9 | 8.6 | 278.3 | 31.9 |
| 1980 | 318.4 | 291.8 | 8.5 | 283.3 | 35.1 |
| 1981 | 326.7 | 298.4 | 8.6 | 289.8 | 36.9 |
| 1982 | 338.7 | 309.2 | 8.6 | 300.6 | 38.1 |
| 1983 | 346.9 | 312.1 | 8.6 | 303.5 | 43.4 |
| 1984 | 359.7 | 309.3 | 8.5 | 300.8 | 58.9 |
| 1985 | 370.6 | 311.9 | 8.3 | 303.6 | 67.0 |
| 1986 | 379.9 | 313.0 | 8.4 | 304.6 | 75.3 |
| 1987 | 390.0 | 317.2 | 8.5 | 308.7 | 81.3 |
| 1988 | | 321.7 | | | |

a. For 1970–1977 values were obtained by subtracting column three from column two.
b. For 1970–1977 values were obtained by subtracting column four from column one.
SOURCES: *Statistical Yearbook of China*, 1984, 114, and *China Statistical Yearbook*, 1988, 123, 127, and 130.

employees of state farms and the agricultural bureaucracy. It has been assumed that none of these staff and workers are included in the category "collective and individual laborers in rural areas."

During the first half of the 1970s, while the Cultural Revolution was still a significant force influencing economic decisions, less than 2 percent of the rural labor force was engaged in activities outside of agriculture. Relaxation of the control of the activities of farm people apparently started in 1976, with a major change occurring in 1978 when nonagricultural employment increased to 31.5 million or 10.2 percent of the rural labor force. The growth of nonagricultural employment continued through 1982 at a relatively slow rate and then grew much faster, with a major increase in 1984 and continued rapid growth through 1987.

From 1977 to 1988 agricultural employment increased by 24 million, while the number of workers in the rural areas increased by 88 million. The income position of farm families was positively and significantly affected by the increase in nonagricultural income opportunities. Had it been necessary to provide for 65 or so million additional workers in agriculture, farm family incomes would have been adversely affected for two reasons. First, nonfarm positions provided significantly higher incomes per day than employment in agriculture, leading many millions to shift to nonfarm work. Second, the marginal product from work in agriculture would have fallen sharply if employment had increased by more than 20 percent from its actual level.

Table 3 provides a breakdown of nonagricultural employment for collective and individual workers in rural areas for 1978–1987 (employment in agriculture is shown as well). From 1982 through 1987 nonagricultural employment in rural areas increased by 43.2 million, while agricultural employment increased by only 8.1 million.

Job creation in rural areas between 1978 and 1987 was quite remarkable, to put it mildly. A total of 50 million nonagricultural jobs were created, almost entirely by local resources with no contribution from the central government. The creation of 15.6 million industrial jobs, 12.0 million construction jobs, 4.8 million transportation jobs, and 5.6 million jobs in commerce and trade represented a major achievement of local initiative.

The growth in nonagricultural jobs in rural areas continued until at least mid-1989. Village and township enterprises employed "some 100 million people in rural areas," according to a statement made in September 1989 by Chen Yaohang, vice minister of agriculture (FBIS-CHI-89-180, September 19, 1989, 38).

## Changes in Sources of Income of Farm Households

Change in the sources of income of farm households can be looked at in two different ways: by institutional source (Table 4) and by activity. According to Table 4, 66 percent of farm families' incomes in 1978 came from the collective and 27 percent from the household operation (essentially the income from private plots and from raising livestock

TABLE 3 Labor Force of Townships and Villages by Sector, 1978–1987 (millions)

| | 1978 | 1979 | 1980 | 1981 | 1982 | 1983 | 1984 | 1985 | 1986 | 1987 |
|---|---|---|---|---|---|---|---|---|---|---|
| Total | 306.38 | 310.25 | 318.36 | 326.72 | 338.67 | 346.90 | 359.68 | 370.65 | 379.90 | 390.00 |
| Farming, forestry, animal husbandry, fishery, and water conservancy | 274.88 | 278.35 | 283.34 | 289.80 | 300.62 | 303.50 | 300.80 | 303.51 | 304.68 | 308.70 |
| Industry | 17.34 | 17.56 | 19.42 | 19.81 | 20.73 | 21.68 | 25.49 | 37.41 | 31.39 | 32.97 |
| Construction | 2.30 | 2.33 | 2.83 | 2.97 | 3.79 | 4.83 | 8.11 | 11.30 | 13.09 | 14.31 |
| Transportation, posts, and telecommunications | 0.80 | 0.81 | 0.90 | 1.01 | 1.15 | 1.61 | 3.17 | 4.34 | 5.06 | 5.62 |
| Commerce, catering trade, supply and marketing of materials and warehouses | 0.52 | 0.53 | 0.67 | 0.75 | 0.83 | 1.37 | 2.99 | 4.63 | 5.32 | 6.07 |
| Real estate administration, public utilities, residential services, and consultancy services | 0.12 | 0.13 | 0.45 | 0.46 | 0.47 | 0.69 | 1.22 | 0.89 | 1.26 | 1.38 |
| Public health, sports, and social welfare | 1.16 | 1.17 | 1.02 | 0.73 | 0.87 | 0.92 | 0.99 | 1.22 | 1.25 | 1.27 |
| Education, culture, art, radio and television broadcasting | 3.57 | 3.62 | 3.30 | 2.38 | 2.60 | 2.73 | 2.88 | 3.10 | 3.15 | 3.14 |
| Scientific research, comprehensive technical services | — | — | 0.08 | 0.16 | 0.14 | 0.12 | 0.12 | 0.13 | 0.15 | 0.16 |
| Banking, insurance | 0.11 | 0.11 | 0.10 | 0.10 | 0.11 | 0.11 | 0.12 | 0.12 | 0.14 | 0.16 |
| Governments, parties, and organizations | 0.37 | 0.37 | 0.37 | 0.36 | 0.34 | 0.55 | 0.74 | 0.81 | 1.03 | 1.20 |
| Other | 5.21 | 5.27 | 5.88 | 8.19 | 7.02 | 8.79 | 13.05 | 13.19 | 13.38 | 15.02 |

SOURCE: *China Statistical Yearbook*, 1988, 142.

and poultry). The remainder (7 percent) came from gifts, public welfare funds, the state budget, and remittances from family members who worked outside the village. By 1983 the income from collectives had declined to 11.6 percent of the total and the share from household production had increased to 79 percent. These relative shares have remained roughly constant since that year. The still significant share of income from collectives is concentrated in the suburban areas of large cities such as Beijing, Shanghai, and Tianjin, where many of the communes were more industrial than agricultural.

Sources of income by type of activity are given in Table 5 (SYOC 1988, 733). Given the shifts in employment described earlier, the share of income derived from agriculture has declined over time, from 85 percent in 1978 to 65 percent in 1987. The percentage from nonagricultural production increased from 7 percent to 25 percent over the same period. These rapid shifts indicate the distortionary effects of the com-

TABLE 4 Net per Capita Income of Peasants by Source, Selected Years, 1978–1987

| | 1978 | 1980 | 1983 | 1984 | 1985 | 1986 | 1987 |
|---|---|---|---|---|---|---|---|
| Average net per capita income (yuan) | 133.57 | 191.33 | 309.77 | 355.33 | 397.6 | 423.76 | 462.55 |
| From collective | 88.53 | 108.37 | 36.06 | 35.33 | 33.37 | 36.15 | 42.09 |
| From new rural economic union | | | 0.88 | 2.85 | 3.69 | 2.92 | 3.49 |
| From household production | 35.79 | 62.55 | 244.66 | 285.44 | 322.53 | 345.28 | 383.57 |
| From other non-borrowed income | 9.25 | 20.41 | 28.17 | 31.71 | 38.01 | 39.41 | 33.40 |
| Proportion (%, net income = 100) | | | | | | | |
| From collective | 66.3 | 56.6 | 11.6 | 10.0 | 8.4 | 8.5 | 9.1 |
| From new rural economic union | | | 0.3 | 0.8 | 0.9 | 0.7 | 0.8 |
| From household production | 26.8 | 32.7 | 79.0 | 80.3 | 81.1 | 81.5 | 82.9 |
| From other non-borrowed income | 6.9 | 10.7 | 9.1 | 8.9 | 9.6 | 9.3 | 7.2 |

SOURCE: *China Statistical Yearbook*, 1988, 732.

mune system and the associated controls over the family's use of their labor. Many of the restrictions on nonagricultural activities were imposed so that farm people would be forced to devote their time and energy to the collective activity. Such views were so firmly held that in a number of villages fruit trees and vegetable crops grown in the house yards of families were destroyed to prevent the diversion of time and effort, although ideology probably also played a role. Among some rabid communists such activities were thought to represent capitalist activities and thus had to be prevented.

Rural reforms had many positive consequences: rapid growth of farm output, large increases in the incomes of farm households, and a substantial transfer of labor out of agriculture into the more productive

TABLE 5 Net per Capita Income of Peasants by Activity, Selected Years, 1978–1987

| | 1978 | 1980 | 1983 | 1984 | 1985 | 1986 | 1987 |
|---|---|---|---|---|---|---|---|
| Average net per capita income (yuan) | 133.57 | 191.33 | 309.77 | 355.33 | 397.6 | 423.76 | 462.55 |
| Net income, productive | 122.86 | 166.39 | 272.91 | 315.06 | 350.07 | 374.68 | 418.35 |
| Agricultural production[a] | 113.47 | 149.62 | 221.77 | 250.36 | 263.81 | 278.98 | 300.79 |
| Nonagricultural production[b] | 9.39 | 16.77 | 51.15 | 64.70 | 86.26 | 95.70 | 117.56 |
| Net income, nonproductive[c] | 10.71 | 24.94 | 36.86 | 40.27 | 47.53 | 49.08 | 44.20 |
| Proportion (%; net income = 100) | | | | | | | |
| Net income, productive | 92.0 | 87.0 | 88.1 | 88.7 | 88.0 | 88.4 | 90.4 |
| Agricultural production[a] | 85.0 | 78.2 | 71.6 | 70.5 | 66.3 | 65.8 | 65.0 |
| Nonagricultural production[b] | 7.0 | 8.8 | 16.5 | 18.2 | 21.7 | 22.6 | 25.4 |
| Net income, nonproductive[c] | 8.0 | 13.0 | 11.9 | 11.3 | 12.0 | 11.6 | 9.6 |

a. Net income of peasants who engage in farming, forestry, animal husbandry, a sideline occupation, or fishery.

b. Net income of peasants who engage in rural industry, construction, transport, commerce, or catering trade.

c. Income, both in cash and in kind, sent or brought back by those working elsewhere; income received from collective accumulation fund and public welfare fund; and income received from the state budget.

SOURCE: *China Statistical Yearbook*, 1988, 733.

earning opportunities created within rural communities. By encouraging the growth of markets in both rural and urban areas and permitting farm people to buy and sell without being accused of speculation or punished for obtaining "unearned" income, the government greatly expanded the opportunities available to farm people for the effective utilization of their income and talents. Farmers also were permitted to own the "means of production" such as tractors and trucks. Thus, they greatly enhanced the capacity of the transportation system in rural areas.

As of mid-1989, however, the reforms were still incomplete. A number of important issues, such as agreement on the ownership of land or on the security of the use rights to land assigned under the responsibility system, have remained unresolved after nearly a decade of reform. The central government has sharply reduced its investment in agriculture and rural communities, using funds instead for bigger and better apartments for urban families and bigger and better offices for urban bureaucrats.

## CHAPTER 4

# Urban and Industrial Reforms

It was easier to summarize the rural and agricultural reforms than it will be to describe the urban and industrial reforms; the latter have been much more limited and hesitant. The industrial reforms have included nothing comparable to the adoption of the household responsibility system or the abolition of the communes.

The rural reforms seem to have been based on a clearer vision of the future than the industrial reforms. Even so, as noted earlier, there did not appear to be a clear-cut blueprint for the rural reforms as of 1978, and the same applied to the urban and industrial reforms. Much of what followed was adaptation of what had seemed to work and what had generated popular support. Apparently, there was no single measure or group of coordinated measures that served to push ahead industrial reforms at a rapid pace. A number of measures were either implemented half-heartedly, such as breaking the "iron rice bowl" or applying the bankruptcy laws for state enterprises, or were soon withdrawn because of unwanted consequences, such as the early efforts at giving enterprise managers greater authority to determine output.

## 1978 Communiqué of the Communist Party of China

The famous communiqué of the Third Plenary Session of the Eleventh Central Committee of the Communist Party of China (December 22, 1978) was the genesis of the rural reforms but provided only the most general guidelines for the urban and industrial reforms. An important general statement that guided subsequent reform efforts dealt with the issue of undue concentration of decision-making authority in the economy:

> One of the serious shortcomings in the structure of economic management in our country is the overconcentration of authority, and it is necessary to shift it under guidance from the leadership to lower authorities and industrial and agricultural enterprises will have greater power of decision in management under guidance of unified state planning. . . . (Liu and Wu 1986, 569).

The same paragraph noted that the functions of the party, government, and enterprise should be separated and that it was necessary "to put a stop to the substitution of Party for government and the substitution of government for enterprise administration. . . . " Except for a brief discussion of the need to reduce the number of meetings and the amount of paperwork "to raise work efficiency, and conscientiously adopt the practices of examination, reward and punishment, promotion and demotion," there were no guidelines or discussions about how the urban and industrial reforms were to be carried out.

## New Leap Forward, 1978

The highly ambitious and unrealistic ten-year development program put forward in 1978 by Hua Guofeng, who had replaced Mao as chairman of the party upon Mao's death in 1976, was the first reform effort after Mao. The plan attempted to redress the disorganization of the economy that had occurred during the Cultural Revolution when the central government had lost much of its control over industrial enterprises to provincial and local governments. The role of central planning was to be reinforced, and financial resources, especially the depreciation allowances that had been retained by enterprises during the Cultural Revolution, were once again to be recaptured by the center.

Harry Harding (1987, 55) has described the basic nature of what was proposed:

> As set out in his ten-year development program introduced in 1978, Hua's strategy assumed that higher rates of growth could be stimulated by political stability, higher investment, and greater incentives, without any basic structural reforms. Accelerating mechanization and reestablishing material incentives for peasant families would stimulate agricultural output. Higher levels of state investment, a crash program of importing technology, heavy reliance on foreign loans, and increases in urban wages would increase industrial productivity. Under Hua's leadership, the rate of investment rose to 36.5 percent of national output in 1978, higher than any time in the history of the People's Republic except for the Great Leap Forward.

That Hua did not perceive the need for institutional reform was made clear by his adherence to the "two whatevers" (see Chapter 1). He supported, for example, "learning from Dazhai," although, as noted earlier, Dazhai was not an appropriate example. According to one objective established, by 1980 a third of the counties would be of the Dazhai type, with emphasis on investment projects requiring large amounts of labor and on egalitarianism in the distribution of income. As late as November 1978 it had been proposed that by the following spring a tenth of the production brigades practice unified accounting "to pave the way for another step forward in the transition to communism" (Liu and Wu 1986, 431). Agriculture was to be fully mechanized by the end of the century, an unrealistic and unreasonable objective. Even though Hua still retained his positions as chairman of the Communist party and premier, the December 1978 decisions with respect to agriculture reversed virtually all of Hua's program for agriculture.

The fact that the 1978 plenum provided no new initiatives for industry—and apparently left it to the basic presumptions of Hua's ten-year development plan to serve as the basis for industrial and urban improvement—may well have been caused by the internal disarray within the Communist party resulting from Deng's eventually successful effort to displace and replace Hua. In 1980 Hua was forced to give up the premiership, and by mid-1981 he had lost the party chairmanship. A year later he was forced off the Politburo (Harding 1987, 64).

By 1980 it was clear that the economy was running into major difficulties as a result of unrealistic targets, a large negative foreign trade balance, and a substantial government deficit. The budget deficit could be traced to some degree to the one set of important reforms affecting the industrial structure, promulgated in July 1979. These reforms were intended to reduce central control over the day-to-day operations of enterprises, to introduce capital charges, to require payment of interest on funds borrowed, and to permit enterprises to retain part of their profits and to retain the part of the depreciation charges they were paying into the state budget (Naughton 1985, 226). While these measures were intended to apply to a limited number of enterprises, as had happened in other cases, what was intended to be an experimental program became implemented broadly. By a year later, 6,600 industrial enterprises that accounted for 60 percent of the gross value of industrial output and 70 percent of industrial profits were participating in the schemes (Liu and Wu 1986, 442). As Naughton (1985, 230–233) pointed out, the reforms were only very partially implemented; only the profit and depreciation retentions seem to have been almost fully implemented. Enterprises did not receive substantial discretion in their day-to-day operations or an increase in their autonomy. Nor was much use made of the provision that enterprises should pay a charge related to their fixed capital. In late 1980 it was announced that profit-sharing was to be extended to all state enterprises by the end of 1981, and apparently this was achieved. By letting some of the profits and depreciation allowances remain at the discretion of enterprises and local authorities, the government encouraged an increasing percentage of fixed investment at the local level, with the percentage increasing from 34 percent in 1978, to 49 percent in 1980, and to 58 percent in 1981.

Much of the increase in local investment—more than 15 billion yuan between 1978 and 1981 (Naughton 1985, 229)—apparently came out of funds that in earlier years would have gone to support the central budget. In any case, after June 1980 profit remittances to the state budget declined sharply, and a substantial budget deficit emerged. In 1980 central government budget revenues were 108.5 billion yuan, with a deficit of 12.8 billion yuan. This followed a much larger deficit of 17.1 billion yuan in 1979, caused, at least in part, by the war with Vietnam (SYOC 1988, 665). Included in the 1981 revenues were 4.3 billion yuan derived from "debts and borrowings"; thus the real deficit that year was 17.1 billion yuan. No borrowing was evident for 1978, however, when there was a modest budget surplus.

The revenues from enterprise profits and industrial and commercial taxes declined by 7.7 billion yuan between 1978 and 1980. The enterprise income allocated to the budget apparently declined for reasons other than the industrial reforms related to income sharing and retention of depreciation by enterprises. In the *Statistical Yearbook of China* (1988, 667), a garbled footnote states that from 1980 through 1984 enterprise income that was included in the state budget was significantly less than actual enterprise income because of "heavy losses by foreign trade enterprises and grain enterprises." The losses of grain enterprises in 1980 included 4.3 billion yuan in price subsidies for imported commodities; it may have included other losses as well.

But loss of revenue did not seem to have been the major factor in causing the deficit, since the 1980 revenue was only 3.6 billion yuan below what was realized in 1978. More important in absolute terms was the increase in expenditures of more than 10 billion yuan from 1978 to 1980, including perhaps that part of the increase in the price subsidies charged to the state budget. The 14.8 billion increase in such subsidies between 1978 and 1980 resulted from the failure to increase the retail prices of grain and vegetable oil when procurement prices were increased in 1979 and the difference between the costs of five imported commodities and what was realized from their sale at the low and subsidized consumer prices (SYOC 1988, 681).

The shock of the large budget deficits in 1979 and 1980 and a foreign trade deficit of $3.3 billion total for the two years induced the government to put a halt to the industrial reforms and adopt a deflationary policy that included a reduction of 40 percent in planned budgeted investments. The short-run effect of the deflationary policy was to reduce government revenue, creating a potential increase in the deficit rather than a reduction. By late 1981 the deflationary policies had been relaxed. But a new twist was introduced in 1981 in response to the confusion that resulted from the efforts to cool off the economy earlier in the year. In a profit-contracting arrangement put into effect in early 1981, the central authorities established profit targets for enterprises. As Naughton noted (1985, 234), the profit targets sent out were unrealistically high, given the deflationary policy. Consequently, enterprises refused to accept the targets on the grounds they were impossible.

The profit-contracting scheme primarily affected the smaller firms; the majority of the large enterprises remained under the profit retention program. The profit-contracting arrangements negotiated with each enterprise involved establishing a base level of profits that was to be turned over to the state in its entirety. Enterprises were then allowed to retain 20–100 percent of their profits in excess of the base amount. Although the negotiating process was difficult and time-consuming and the results often considered quite arbitrary, this scheme spread rapidly, and by early 1982 more than 80 percent of state enterprises had adopted it. The enterprises may have been the better bargainers since profit retention increased and budget revenue fell below the goals.

By the end of 1982 yet another approach to government finance was agreed on—a series of four taxes. Three were quite straightforward: a tax on fixed and circulating capital, the existing sales tax and an income tax. The fourth tax, called an adjustment tax, was instituted to equalize the economic circumstances of various enterprises where differences in profitability existed for reasons unrelated to management ability and organization. Profits of equally well-managed and motivated enterprises can vary widely because of different price relationships between outputs and inputs, location, and natural resource endowments. The latter was particularly important for mining enterprises (Naughton 1985, 241). In effect, the adjustment tax was required to offset some of the effects of a distorted price system and the absence of markets for natural resources, including urban land.

Thus in a span of only three years, enterprises had been confronted by four different types of financial relationships with the central government: submission of all profits and depreciation, retention of part of profits, profit contracting, and a tax on profits. It seems clear that no systematic financial plan had been agreed on when it was decided that reform of the urban and industrial economies was required. Furthermore, there was no general plan of reform broad enough to encompass all of the changes required to improve significantly the functioning of the industrial economy. Some of the partial reforms, such as increasing enterprise autonomy, either were not carried out universally or led to inappropriate outcomes because of irrational prices and wage and employment requirements that left enterprises little able to use resources efficiently. Unless an enterprise knows the value to the economy and society of both its outputs and inputs, it cannot use those resources to produce outputs that maximize the benefit. The reforms did not provide the managers of enterprises with such knowledge during the period under review.

### Urban Reforms of 1984

Not until October 1984 was a reasonably detailed program of reforms of the urban economy put forward. Retail prices were relatively stable in 1982 and 1983, the foreign trade balance was significantly positive for the same two years, and, although the budget deficit (including borrowing) remained at a relatively high level, it seemed to have stabilized at 12 billion yuan. In addition, the share of accumulation in national income had been brought below 30 percent, and the share of light industry in total industrial output had been increased to more than 50 percent in 1982 and 1983 from 43 percent in 1978 (SYOC 1988). Finally, Deng Xiaoping appeared to be firmly in control of both the party and the government.

According to economist Wu Jinglian, the 1984 urban reforms applied to urban areas the same principles that were embodied in the overall rural reforms that followed the Third Plenary Session in 1978. He noted that the rural reforms included the contract system,

> delegating powers as well as conceding interests to peasant households. This worked as expected—it released the energy of tens of millions of peasants and changed in a short time the face of rural areas. The overall urban reform launched in 1984 was conducted much on the same line: delegating powers and conceding interests to individuals. (FBIS-CHI-88-221, November 16, 1988, 46)

But just as the industrial reforms that were promulgated in July 1979 were postponed and largely ignored because of difficulties with macroeconomic management of the economy—large government budget and foreign account deficits—the 1984 reforms met essentially the same fate. According to Wu:

> . . . near the end of the year abnormal conditions appeared. Localities stepped up industrial growth, clamored and raced with one another to double their outputs, and expanded the target quotas at every administrative tier. Investment and consumption expanded. There were enormous money supplies in all 4 quarters of the year and extremely unstable price levels. (FBIS-CHI-88-221, November 16, 1988, 46)

In 1985 the cost of living index for urban workers increased by 12 percent, the largest increase in more than two decades. Imports exceeded exports by 45 billion yuan. The share of accumulation in national income increased from 31.5 percent in 1984 to 35.2 percent in 1985. Once again, it was decided that the time was not propitious for carrying out reforms of the urban economy. Consequently, as of mid-1989 most of the reform measures envisaged in the 1984 statement had not been carried out.

A brief look at the major objectives of the 1984 reforms as adopted by the Communist Party of China on October 20, 1984, may help explain what has been accomplished since that time. The first objective was to reduce the role of government agencies, including the planning agency, and to expand the role of the enterprises in the conduct of economic production and distribution: "In short, the enterprise should be truly made a relatively independent economic entity and should become a producer and operator of socialist commodity production that is independent and responsible for its own profit and loss and capable of transforming itself and that acts as a legal person with certain rights and duties" (Liu and Wu 1986, 679).

The second objective was to reform the planning system but not to abolish planning. While it was stated that China's economy was "on the whole a planned economy," it also was noted that such a label did "not necessarily mean the preponderance of mandatory planning, both mandatory and guidance planning being its specific forms." Mandatory planning was to be applied to "major products which have a direct bearing on the national economy and the people's livelihood and which have to be allocated and distributed by the state. . . . " What these products were was not indicated, but the next sentence noted that "other products and economic activities which are far more numerous should either come under guidance planning or be left entirely to the operation of the market . . . " (Liu and Wu 1986, 682–83).

The third objective was to reform prices and to replace the irrational prices. It was recognized that the other important reforms could not be carried out effectively without price reform. As noted by Liu and Wu (1986, 683), "The various aspects of the reform in economic structure, including planning and wage systems, depend to a large extent on reform of the price system." The very important point is made that in the absence of price reform "it will be impossible to assess correctly the performance of enterprises, ensure the smooth circulation of goods between urban and rural areas, promote technological advances and rationalize the production mix and consumption patterns." A Chicago economist could not have said it better!

The fourth objective of the reforms was to separate government from enterprise functions. It was stated that henceforth government departments at any level would "not manage or operate enterprises directly" (Liu and Wu 1986, 687). This part of the document was particularly difficult to read and understand. It seemed evident, however, that enterprise autonomy could not be achieved as long as government bureaucrats were directly engaged in managing enterprises.

The fifth objective of the reforms was to introduce the economic responsibility system to urban enterprises, thereby linking "the incomes of workers and staff members with their job performance." This aspect of the reforms represented recognition of the success of the responsibility system in rural and farm areas. It was emphasized that modern enterprises, with their minute division of labor and continuity in production, require "a unified, authoritative and highly efficient system to direct production and conduct operations and management. This calls for a system of the manager or director assuming full responsibility." The text goes on to state that the party organizations in enterprises "should actively support directors in exercizing their authority in giving direction to production and operations. . . ." But, since the party is to "guarantee and supervise the implementation of the principles and policies of the Party and the state," it may be quite difficult to determine whether the local party organization, especially the secretary, is interfering with the prerogatives of the director (Liu and Wu, 690).

Because little or no progress has been made in achieving any one of these five objectives of the economic reforms agreed to on October 20, 1984, there has been little systematic reform of the urban economy. The disarray of the economy that caused the party and government to go slow with the reforms in 1985 has tended to increase as time has passed. In the year and a half before June 1989 the government lost macroeconomic control of the economy. Inflation was at a high level, perhaps reaching 30 percent, in large part because the banking system lost control of the supply of loans and of money.

## Failure to Reform Prices

Although there has not been a general or systematic reform of prices, some measures have been taken since 1978 in an effort to increase the role of the market. Because all the efforts have been partial in nature, the consequences generally have not been the ones desired. In the discussion that follows, no attempt is made to consider all of the efforts to effect partial price reform; the primary intent is to illustrate what can happen with some price reform efforts.

But first a few words about rural price reforms are in order, if for no other reason than that urban dwellers are affected by the prices of farm products. Rural price reforms and changes have performed reasonably well. In part this has been because the farm prices that prevailed in 1978 were not as far away from equilibrium prices as many industrial prices. This may have resulted from the difference in the economic organization of agriculture and of industry. Although industrial enterprises were state owned and the government absorbed all profits *and* losses incurred, industrial prices could deviate wildly from the prices that would have equated supply and demand. But because the communes, brigades, and production teams were independent organizations without a direct claim against the government to cover their losses, the prices paid for farm products had to be sufficient to cover costs of purchased inputs and to pay for food and shelter for most of the peasants. The government did provide some relief in the way of food or reduced taxes when there was a crop disaster, but this affected only a minority of peasants in a given year. Consequently, purchase prices for farm products, even though there were required delivery quotas, bore a significant relationship to economic reality. This was not the case, however, for industrial prices.

The government has had a variety of prices for farm products. For a time there was the possibility of four different prices: the quota price for required deliveries, a higher price for deliveries in excess of the quota, a negotiated price, and a (relatively) free market price. Thus, there was a flow of information about the price situation for the affected commodities. Some prices of farm products—for example, pork, poultry, eggs, fruits, and vegetables—have been freed of price controls, at least for a period of time. When price inflation became serious in 1988, however, a number of cities reimposed price ceilings on several food products. There is considerable autonomy with regard to such policies in China; in this respect China is far from a monolith.

One of the early industrial price reforms—use of a dual price system—may have been an effort to duplicate the effects of the introduction of free market prices for part of farm output. Its supporters hoped this system would provide an approach to a market price regime. The idea, which was implemented to some degree as early as 1981, was that part of an enterprise's output would be sold at a price fixed by the state, while the remainder would be sold at a negotiated price. The part of the output sold at a fixed price would then be allocated to enterprises using the product as an input.

If as industrial output has grown over the years, control over credit and money supply had limited inflation to 2–3 percent annually, the dual price system might be meeting the objectives of its promoters. Under these circumstances, the negotiated or market prices probably would have declined over time if they had started out as a high multiple of the fixed price. Unfortunately, in reality the spread between fixed and negotiated or market prices has increased in an inflationary situation, and the dual price system has become a source of distortions rather than a solution to the problem of price reform.

Wu Jinglian noted that when the dual or double-tier system was put forward in 1981, ideology influenced the outcome (FBIS-CHI-88-221, November l6, 1988, 48). The double-tier system represented a compromise that was required at the time. But, he argued, when the ideological obstacles had been eliminated by 1984, "our understanding continued to remain in the double-tier price system. Some went so far as to claim this was to be the path of reform—with Chinese characters. In fact, double-tier price system works against the basic requirement of the market: equal competition." He argued that with the system, an enterprise that makes profits "cannot tell if that is a result of good prices or sound business operation. If we cannot distinguish a good enterprise from a bad one, there will be no way to ask one to carry out the practice of shouldering its own profits and losses; much less to form an environment where only the fittest enterprises survive." The last point, of course, refers to any situation in which prices are seriously distorted, whether there is one or several prices for the same product.

Wu also concluded that the system has had an unintended effect: it breeds corruption. Whoever has control over the allocation of the quota amounts available at the low fixed price possesses a valuable asset; and all too often the temptation is seized to realize something on the value of that asset. Much of the corruption that exists in the Chinese economy results from the irrationality of the price system. Many individuals or enterprises are in a position to obtain products at the low fixed state prices and to sell them at market prices that are substantially higher. But such temptation exists whenever the fixed prices are substantially below market clearing prices; corruption does not require a double-tier price system.

Wu's point that under the double-tier price system you cannot tell whether an enterprise is efficient or not is borne out by personal experience. While visiting a small manufacturing plant that processed a product that accounted for a relatively high percentage of the value of the final product, I learned that the plant operated an average of only twenty days a month. It appeared to be reasonably profitable, however, and paid competitive wages. Inquiry revealed that the plant had a quota at a low fixed price for the product that it processed and that the quota was enough for twenty days' operation. If the plant had purchased the same product at the higher market price, it would have lost money. Thus, it behaved rationally by not incurring losses. This example, however, leaves Wu's question unanswered: Would this enterprise have survived if the price of the input had been where supply equaled demand at a single price?

### Labor Utilization

It has been recognized for some time that three serious problems affect the utilization of labor in state enterprises, and in China each of these problems has been subject to reform efforts, albeit largely unsuccessful ones. The reasons for these shortcomings vary, but there are two common threads. The first is that each reform has been considered in isolation; for example, there has not been an overall program for the relations between employer and employee nor for the responsibilities the government may have in case of unemployment. The second is that even the fairly modest reforms proposed have been resisted strongly either by workers or by politically oriented groups.

**"Iron rice bowl."** Economists in China have long recognized that the conditions associated with employment, compensation, and assignment of workers are a major barrier to efficient production. One of the conditions of employment is the so-called iron rice bowl. As Xue Muqiao (1981, 210) has described it: "Workers are hired but not fired, promoted but not demoted, a phenomenon which we call an 'iron rice bowl.'" In effect, a worker receives tenure the first day on the job. After that, it is virtually impossible to fire anyone who is employed by a state or urban collective enterprise. Repeated inquiries on visits to a number of state and collective enterprises have not turned up cases in which a worker has been fired. Occasionally, there have been reports of a worker being suspended for periods of time, but even then the worker is paid enough to live on. There have been repeated statements about the need to limit severely the iron rice bowl, but it appeared to be little easier to fire a worker in 1989 than it was in 1978.

**"Everyone eating out of the same big pot."** Under socialism, pay should be "to each according to his work." This principle has served as a guideline for wage policy in China, but for several reasons it has failed to provide a wage or incentive system that motivates employees and employers to make efficient and productive use of labor resources. There are a number of reasons why an approach to reward that appears to be the same as the one used in a market enterprise system has failed to provide an adequate incentive to achieve efficient use of labor. One reason for its failure in China is that "to each according to his work" has been interpreted to refer to work input rather than to the productivity of the work. But the work input has not been well monitored, if monitored at all. Consequently, even the relationship between work input and pay has been weak.

For some time piece-rate systems and bonuses were used to reward productivity in some enterprises. But, according to Xue (1981, 83), the Gang of Four "called piece wages and bonuses revisionist practices and abolished them, dampening the enthusiasms of the staff and workers." There does not appear to have been a return to piece-rate systems in state enterprises since the fall of the Gang of Four. Thus after 1965, whatever relationship there may have been between worker productivity and pay in earlier years no longer existed. As the economist Dong Fureng (1982, 73) wrote: "A worker's performance bears no relationship to his job security nor to his income. These conditions stifle the development of the worker's incentive and bring about a great deal of waste in the utilization of financial, material and labour resources."

Since Dong Fureng wrote the above in 1982, has anything changed? As of 1982, the spread in wages in state enterprises was relatively small, and the level of pay did not depend on the profitability of the enterprise in which an individual was employed. In the early 1980s a wage bonus system was introduced to permit enterprise directors to reward either individual workers or groups of workers who had increased their output in a cost-efficient manner. The bonuses were to be used to create a relationship between productivity and pay. Based on a number of visits, I observed, however, that bonuses were not used to differentiate pay according to performance within a given enterprise. Instead, when bonuses were paid, they were distributed on an egalitarian basis. As a consequence of all this, the connection between productivity and reward remains nebulous and ineffective in providing incentives to work hard and well. In this area the reform efforts have failed to produce significant results.

In an article published in late 1988, Dong Fureng discussed the influence of the old system—that is, the system that prevailed for two decades up to the time of Mao's death:

> The old system is a complete system with a very strong and rigid structure of interests. Any reform item will, more or less, change the former structure of economic interests. Although many social interest groups support reform, it is not easy to change the existing structure of economic interests. In the course of carrying out reform it will be resisted by the old economic and political structure and their corresponding ideology. Sometimes the resistance manifests itself in such a way that the reform becomes something that can be tolerated by the old system. Sometimes the content of the old system is injected into the new covering of reform, so that reform loses shape. For example, in carrying out reform in our country, we are restoring the bonus system that was once abolished in order to overcome egalitarianism in distribution and give play to the role of the stimulation of economic interests. This reform is naturally needed and correct. However, in the course of implementing the bonus system, it loses shape. The "bonus" system exists in form only, because it is distributed in an equal way. The distribution of bonuses is resisted by the former rigid structure of interests. Those who failed to do their work well are not willing to get less, whereas those who have done well do not dare to get more. (FBIS-CHI-88-251, December 30, 1988, 32)

Dong's statement carries a striking truth that is relevant to any reform effort, whether in a socialized or market economy or in a dictatorship or a democracy. The existing system has created economic interests that will be affected adversely by any change in the system. It is true that there may be many who will gain from the change, but, first, their gain is uncertain and, second, it may make them objects of jealousy and social pressure. Thus, reform is always difficult, and very often specific reforms are distorted and largely nullified by being coopted by those who would lose if the reforms were carried out effectively. The difficulty encountered in reforming U.S. energy, trade, or agriculture policies goes far in explaining why the much more drastic reforms required in China often have not been carried out.

The negative incentive to work effectively has been removed by the iron rice bowl; it is virtually impossible to fire an employee in a state or collective enterprise. Malingering or sloppy work is not sufficient to cause one to be fired, and positive incentives have been minimized because the efforts to reward productivity have failed due to the continued adherence to egalitarianism in urban enterprises.

**Assignment of workers.** Until the return to the cities of most of the young people and workers who had been sent to the countryside during the Cultural Revolution, China had achieved something very close to full employment in the urban economy through a system of worker assignments. After an individual had completed schooling, he or she was assigned to an enterprise. Neither the individual nor the enterprise had anything to say about the assignment, nor did there seem to be much effort to relate the qualifications of the assigned individuals to the skills needed by the enterprise. This system resulted in excessive employment in terms of numbers and inefficient use of much of the labor.

In the 1980s efforts were made to revise the worker assignment system and to introduce a contract system to replace the iron rice bowl. New employees (old employees were exempted from the contract system) were given a contract for a specified number of years, in which some of the important conditions of employment were specified. Theoretically at least, employees who malingered or had records of absenteeism could be dismissed by not renewing their contracts.

The contract system has evolved rather slowly, but it continues to be implemented. As of April 1988 7.5 million workers in state-owned enterprises or 7.8 percent of all such workers had such contracts (FBIS-CHI-89-014, January 24, 1989, 45). Contrary to expectations and intent, some of the newly recruited employees of state-owned enterprises are permanent workers and some are contract workers, leading to a dual employment system that promises to hinder future employment reform. By July 1989 the number of contract workers had increased to 10.5 million out of total employment of 99.3 million in state owned enterprises (FBIS-CHI-89-185, September 26, 1989, 44).

The term "contract worker" can be used in several different senses (the complex nature of labor contracts are well described by Michael Korzec [1988]). As used in this chapter contract worker refers to what might be called more appropriately a contract system worker. These are primarily urban workers employed in state enterprises within the structure of the state plan. At least two other categories of urban workers have employment contracts of limited duration: temporary workers and seasonal workers. The latter may include both urban and rural residents who work in such seasonal enterprises as canning plants and sugarcane processing. But the largest number of people to whom the term "contract worker" can be applied are the workers contracted from the countryside or peasants who work for state and collective enterprises in urban areas. These workers retain their villages as their residence, and they have none of the privileges and fringe benefits of urban workers, who may be either permanent workers or contract system workers. In particular, the contract workers from the countryside do not have access to rationed grain at subsidized prices. The situation is both complex and confusing.

In a radio broadcast in late June 1989 (FBIS-CHI-89-128, July 6, 1989, 61), it was implied that some contract workers have been dismissed for failing to meet the conditions of their employment: "Resignation and dismissal, which used to be a rare and embarrassing state for Chinese workers, have become common in some Chinese cities now. . . . " While noting that 14,000 employees resigned in 1988, the broadcast said no further word about dismissals nor, obviously, gave any estimate of the number of workers dismissed. It seems a reasonable interpretation that the number of dismissals was significantly less than 14,000 out of the labor force in state enterprises of almost 100 million.

One reason enterprises are reluctant to release or fire employees (who are greatly resistant to the idea themselves) is that an important reform is lacking. When all new entrants to the labor force were being assigned and full employment was guaranteed, unemployment insurance or payments and other related social welfare programs were not necessary because officially there was no unemployment. And because enterprises were responsible for all aspects of the lives of their employees—housing, health, schooling—there was no need for universal social welfare programs. Consequently, the dismissal of a worker has major ramifications and thus almost never happens, even when there is very great provocation in terms of absenteeism and malingering.

## Industrial Contract Responsibility System

The success of the contract responsibility system in agriculture led to its adoption by industrial and other urban enterprises. As mentioned earlier, in the brief period from 1980 to 1982 enterprises were faced with four different types of financial relationships with the central government. The contract responsibility system, which apparently became universal in mid-1987, was a part of the effort to determine the amount of revenue that each enterprise would turn over to the government, to give enterprises some independence from the day-to-day intervention of government bureaucracy, and to give enterprises and local government authorities responsibility for their finances.

The contracts themselves cover many aspects of the operation of an enterprise, including the establishment of quotas for taxes and profits and for consumption per unit of output of energy and raw materials. Some evidence indicates that the contracts focus primarily on the amount of taxes to be delivered, but, in principle, the contracts can, and some probably do, include output levels and mix, new investment, repair, and rehabilitation.

Liu Guosheng, a reporter for the *People's Daily*, noted that the separation of government from enterprise functions has not been fully solved: "There have been too many cases of the state unnecessarily intervening, and the enterprises have found it difficult to operate autonomously; . . . impositions, levies and inspections from various quarters are many and frequent, which the enterprises can hardly bear, and effective measures to improve this situation are sadly lacking. . . ." (FBIS-CHI-89-104, June 1, 1989, 48). Thus, it appears that enterprise reform remains very incomplete, and much more needs to be done before enterprises become both independent and responsive to market forces.

## Growth in Industrial Output

According to Table 6, the overall performance of China's industrial economy as measured by output growth is quite remarkable, equaling or exceeding those of such rapidly growing economies as Japan and South Korea. Except for 1958–1962, the period of the Great Leap Forward, industrial output has grown at a rate of nearly 10 percent annually and in some periods at substantially higher rates.

The 1985–1987 growth rate seems inconsistent with the above observation that the 1984 reforms have been of little significance. The growth rate for 1985–1987 is the highest for any period except 1963–1965, which had a very high growth rate stemming from the recovery from the Great Leap. Since 1985 light industry has grown at a higher rate than heavy industry, reversing the long-run trend that favored heavy industry.

To a considerable degree the rapid growth of industrial output during 1985–1987 represents the success of the rural reforms—particularly the remarkable growth of rural industry—rather than the success

TABLE 6 Annual Growth Rates of Industrial Output, 1952–1987 (percentage)

| | All industry | Light industry | Heavy industry |
|---|---|---|---|
| 1953–1957 | 18.0 | 12.9 | 25.4 |
| 1958–1962 | 3.8 | 1.1 | 6.6 |
| 1963–1965 | 17.9 | 21.2 | 14.9 |
| 1966–1970 | 11.7 | 8.4 | 14.7 |
| 1971–1975 | 9.3 | 8.2 | 10.7 |
| 1976–1980 | 9.6 | 11.5 | 8.2 |
| 1981–1984 | 9.9 | 11.3 | 8.4 |
| 1985–1987 | 16.9 | 17.8 | 15.9 |

SOURCE: *China Statistical Yearbook*, 1988, 36.

of the urban and industrial reforms. The development of rural industry primarily stemmed from the rural reforms that gave substantial autonomy to townships and villages to develop productive activities other than agriculture, forestry, and fishing. In 1983 rural industry accounted for about 12 percent of national industrial output; by 1987 this percentage had doubled to 24 percent. Thus, the rate of growth of rural industry had to be somewhat more than double that of urban industry.

There are problems, however, with the rapid growth in overall industrial output claimed in recent years. The first problem is that it may not have been as rapid as claimed. The State Economic Information Center reported on November 17, 1988, that industrial output growth during the first quarter of 1988 was 12.3 percent—not the 16.7 percent that had been reported. The radio broadcast went on to say: "The center holds that the rapid industrial growth rates registered since 1984 were inflated by an average of 2.5 percent" (FBIS-CHI-88-223, November 18, 1988, 26). Thus, the growth rate of 16.9 percent for 1985–1987 may have been a still highly respectable 14.5 percent. The reasons given for the overestimate are familiar to individuals who have studied centrally planned economies: total output value is calculated in part at current rather than constant prices, and, by changing their packages or specifications, old products are claimed to be new products and are given a higher price, since the prices of new products are generally not under direct state control. And where some enterprises had lateral ties to other enterprises, both enterprises independently counted some of the same increase in output.

Although there is considerable complaint about the quality of output, very little hard information is available. In the 1970s and early 1980s large quantities of unsold goods were counted as output even though no one was willing to buy them. It was reported in 1980 that the accumulated stockpile of rolled steel was 20 million tons or two-thirds the annual output of all kinds of steel and that mechanical and electrical engineering products worth 60 billion yuan had been stockpiled as needed. These stockpiles equaled slightly more than 12 percent of the value of the entire industrial output for 1980 (Wang 1980, 81 and SYOC 1988).

The major defects of Chinese industry, however, perhaps relate to the inefficient use of resources—labor and energy, and other natural resources. The major reasons for inefficient use of labor have been given: lack of incentives, both positive and negative, and the assignment system which has allocated most of the current industrial labor force. Given the existing incentive structure, factory managers do not have the tools required to induce a high level of productivity from their existing labor force, and, given the procedures affecting both firing and hiring, they have equally little opportunity to change the composition of their work force.

The inefficient use of energy, which is often the subject of comment by Chinese officials, results from two factors: low energy prices and the outmoded technology used in most factories. Large numbers of factories still operate with the machinery, equipment, and often Soviet technology (which was not fuel-efficient when it was new) of the 1950s. Many new factories have been built since, but frequently they have been copies of existing factories.

In its 1983 study of the Chinese economy the World Bank (1983, 128) noted that energy use per unit of gross national product (GNP) in China was about three times the average for both low- and middle-income developing countries. One reason given for the high energy intensity of the economy as of the late 1970s was the isolation of the economy for the prior two decades and thus lack of access to the equipment and technology that had resulted in substantial energy savings in the industrial market economies. Just as for labor, enterprise managers have not had the incentives to economize on the use of energy.

The failure to adjust the price of energy to reflect its scarcity has had serious adverse effects upon the Chinese economy. Throughout

China's major industrial areas factories do not have enough electricity to operate a full week and thus must shut down for one or two days each week. An enormous waste is caused by equalizing the demand for and supply of energy in this way; industrial capacity is used inefficiently, and much labor effort is wasted during the days the plants are idled.

Increasing the price of energy is not all that is required to use energy efficiently. The incentive structure that applies to the management of enterprises must reward those who use energy efficiently and punish those who use it inefficiently. As of mid-1989 such an incentive system did not exist.

## Other Urban Reforms

Although a considerable number of other urban reforms—in retail distribution, restaurants, and repair services, for example—have been made (see Chapter 5), in some important aspects of life—such as housing—there have been important improvements but no reform.

In the early 1980s the major department stores and most other stores in the cities were exceedingly crowded; at times one could hardly move in the store. It was as if the after-Christmas sale in a large American department store were being held every day of the year. Incongruously, however, even with these crowds almost all stores closed at 5:00 P.M., and clerks tended to stop serving customers well before that.

The practice of early closing was followed even though the absolute space devoted to retail services was the same in 1980 as in the early 1950s. In 1978 retail stores and shops employed 4.5 million people; in 1952 they employed 7.1 million (SYOC 1984, 377). In those twenty-six years the population had increased by 67 percent. This meant that the number of employees in retailing declined from 1.2 per 100 population to 0.5 per 100. Thus, it should not have been surprising that stores were always crowded with long lines. The long lines were generally not because people were waiting for a particular product that had just become available; rather, they were waiting for service from an often sullen and inattentive retail clerk.

The solution to the crowded conditions in retail stores was an exceedingly simple one: increasing the hours of service. This simple solution was not implemented, however, until almost five years after the reform movement was seriously under way in 1978. Apparently, there was significant resistance to the extension of hours of service because it meant that some personnel had to work during the "inconvenient" dinner and early evening hours. Nevertheless, the change was made in the major cities, though not quite at the same time everywhere, since the city governments apparently had some discretion about what the new hours were and when they were implemented.

The improvement in retail services resulted to a considerable degree from one provision of the rural reforms: permitting farmers to sell directly to urban residents. Urban trade markets were opened in 1979. Although the number of such markets increased quite slowly at first (there were 2,226 such markets in 1979 and 3,591 in 1982), by 1987 the number of such markets in urban areas had grown to 10,908, with substantial growth occurring from 1984 to 1986 (SYOC 1984, 363, and 1988, 637).

Urban trade markets have become a major component of the retail food distribution system. In 1987 sales reached 35 billion yuan or 12.5 percent of all retail sales of food (SYOC 1988, 622 and 637). The markets are a major asset to urban people because they provide access to a much greater variety and a much higher quality of food than that available in the state stores. The state stores had had a monopoly in the provision of food to urban residents, and this was quite evident in the quality of goods and service provided.

Another important reform that improved the lives of urban people was the gradual official acceptance of economic activity by individuals or small collectives in urban areas. By 1978 private economic activity in urban areas had been nearly eliminated. In fact, in both rural and urban areas only 262,000 individuals were engaged in private retailing, catering or food service, and general service trades in a nation of nearly a billion people. Although the rural reforms of 1978 sanctioned private economic activity, its acceptance in urban areas apparently came grudgingly and was resisted in a number of cities with conservative administrations. But apparently two factors were compelling in permitting such activity. The first, and probably most important, was the return to the cities of up to 20 million individuals who had been sent to the countryside during the Cultural Revolution. This return, which began in the late 1970s, created substantial unemployment—euphemistically called "waiting for a position" by the Chinese—which was well beyond the capacity of the state sector to absorb in a reasonable period of time. The second reason was that it was generally recognized that in such activities as restaurants and repair services the state sector was doing a miserable job.

Employment in the individual private sector increased from 262,000 in 1978 to 2.7 million in 1982, 13.7 million in 1985, and 14.8 million in 1987. Employment in collectives, many of which were formed by those returning from the countryside, increased from 3.8 million in 1978 to 9 million in 1987. The general improvement in the capacity of the retailing, food catering, and service trades that occurred from 1978 to 1987 stemmed largely from the development of the private and collective sectors rather than the state sector. Of the 22.2 million total increase in employment in these activities that occurred from 1978 to 1987, only 2.5 million was in the state sector. In catering or food services the number of state employees in 1987 was slightly smaller than in 1978—524,000 compared with 606,000—while total national employment increased from 1 million in 1978 to 4.2 million in 1987 (SYOC 1988, 584). Similarly, almost all of the increase in the service trades was under collective or individual ownership.

The improvement in serving the public in these service sectors was obvious when, with population growth of 12 percent, employment more than quadrupled in these sectors between 1978 and 1987. Much of this increase in employment, however, occurred in rural areas. Employment in private enterprises in urban areas, as measured by the number of individual laborers, is currently relatively modest, and there is obviously significant room for further expansion under appropriate policy situations. In 1987, of the 5.7 million individual laborers in cities, 3.9 million were engaged in retailing, catering, and services. The fact that 14.8 million individuals are employed in these categories nationally demonstrates that approximately two-thirds of such employment is in rural areas.

Urban and industrial economic reforms in China have been partial, incomplete, and often only hesitatingly enforced, and they have not been used to eliminate the major distortions in the economy. Moreover, the effort to decentralize decision making by reducing the role of mandatory plans and supply and labor allocations has generally had little positive effect because the existing controlled prices and wages do not provide adequate guidelines for the efficient use of resources. It is even possible that prices are so distorted that allocating resources in response to them will give a less appropriate output mix than the outputs planned by the central planning agency. The distortion in prices and wages also makes it impossible to judge the efficiency of an enterprise by whether it makes a profit or loss or how large its profits or losses may be. Yet when profits are not possible no matter how hard the employees work and how good the managers are in combining the available resources, forcing a firm into bankruptcy is an inappropriate action. Nor is putting an enterprise on a self-financing basis appropriate since profits are not possible and only apparent failure can result. Price reform is essential for successful economic reforms.

# CHAPTER 5

# Income and Consumption Growth since 1978

The Chinese people have benefited substantially from the economic reforms of 1978–1988. A major part of the strong evidence supporting this statement are the data from annual income and expenditure studies that upheld the conclusion that there was little or no increase in real per capita private consumption from the mid-1950s to 1978.

## Rural Incomes and Consumption

Three sets of data are published by the State Statistical Bureau on rural incomes and consumption: a series on current consumption expenditures in current prices, an index of consumption in so-called comparable prices (these two series are available annually for both rural and urban areas for 1952 to date), and surveys of income and consumption for both peasants and workers or rural and urban populations. These estimates are in current prices.

Unfortunately, the State Statistical Bureau provides very little information about the construction of its various statistical series. This is particularly true of the series dealing with consumption expenditures and income and expenditure surveys. But based on careful comparison of the various series dealing with similar information and some private contacts with workers at the State Statistical Bureau, the conclusions drawn here from the available data should be acceptable interpretations of the underlying facts.

Between 1978 and 1987 it is estimated that the real consumption levels of farm people roughly doubled at an annual growth rate of 8 percent. This estimate is based on two independent sources of information. The first source—increase-in-consumption expenditures from the annual household surveys published by the State Statistical Bureau—revealed that per capita expenditures in current prices increased from 116 yuan in 1978 to 398 yuan in 1987 (SYOC 1988, 733). A large component of expenditures was products that were self-produced and consumed by the farm household, valued in the surveys at current market prices. Using the data on the average market prices for the most important self-produced and home-consumed products—principally grains, pork, poultry, eggs, and vegetable oils—it was possible to construct a price index for the products consumed by farmers. For the products that farmers purchased, national price indexes were used for commodity groups such as clothing, goods for daily use, medicines, and cultural and recreational articles. The price index calculated in this way indicated that the cost of rural consumption items increased by roughly 70–75 percent. When the change in the value of consumption in current prices was deflated by the estimated price increase, the result was that consumption about doubled in real terms.

The second independent source—the State Statistical Bureau's estimate of consumption by peasants in comparable prices—revealed that consumption increased by 101 percent between 1978 and 1987 (SYOC 1988, 711). This is essentially the same result obtained from the surveys of consumption expenditure deflated by the price series that was constructed. The State Statistical Bureau's estimates of per capita consumption of peasants in current prices were 132 yuan in 1978 and 388 yuan in 1987 (SYOC 1988, 710). This compares to 116 yuan and 398 yuan, respectively, from the annual household surveys (SYOC 1988, 733). In one respect, these comparisons are reassuring because of the concern expressed that the annual surveys are biased toward the higher-income areas. The comparisons do not support this conclusion. The fact that the increase in real consumption derived from the household surveys is roughly the same as the increase in peasant consumption in comparable prices is only somewhat reassuring. The comparable result requires that different price series were used to deflate the consumption expenditures. The price series used by the State Statistical Bureau can be derived by comparing the changes in consumption in current prices with the changes in consumption in comparable prices. This calculation gives a rural price increase for consumption goods of 56 percent between 1978 and 1987. This is, perhaps coincidentally, the same as the increase in the cost of living of urban workers and significantly less than my estimate of an increase of 70–75 percent for the rural price increase for the same period.

The important point, however, is that two apparently independently derived data series support the conclusion that real consumption per capita of peasants roughly doubled between 1978 and 1987. This was a remarkable outcome, especially since it followed two decades of no increase in per capita private consumption.

The increase in the amount of rural housing space is roughly consistent with the assumption that the real per capita incomes of the peasant population doubled between 1978 and 1987. The amount of living space per capita almost exactly doubled—from 8.1 square meters in 1978 to 16.0 square meters in 1987 (SYOC 1988, 709). Since the income elasticity of demand for housing seems to approximate unity over a wide range of incomes and circumstances, this change in per capita space is consistent with a doubling of income. The quality of rural housing also improved significantly over the decade, implying an income elasticity for real housing expenditures somewhat greater than unity. Such a high income elasticity of demand may have reflected that, as indicated later, in rural China there was a clear bias in favor of housing construction relative to productive investments tied to the land because of different perceptions of the security of property rights for the two types of investment.

In Chapter 2 the expenditure elasticities of demand for food and the changes in food expenditures as a percentage of total consumption expenditures were used to check the official estimates of changes in consumption for both urban and rural residents for the 1950s to 1978. The conclusion was that the approximate constancy of food expenditures as a share of total consumption expenditures was consistent with little or no change in real consumption and quite inconsistent with the official estimates of 50–100 percent increases in per capita consumption. If the same exercise is undertaken for the period of the reforms, 1978–1987, quite different results are obtained for peasants. In 1978 peasants devoted 68 percent of their expenditures to food. Assuming that the consumption expenditure elasticity of demand is 0.7, an increase in real total consumption expenditures by peasants of 100 percent would be expected to reduce the food expenditure share to 58 percent. The actual expenditure share was 55 percent in 1987. If the income elasticity of demand 0.7 did not change over the period, the 1987 expenditure share was consistent with an increase in real consumption or expenditures of somewhat more than 100 percent. The actual changes in the food expenditure shares between 1978 and 1987 are consistent with either a declining expenditure elasticity of demand over time or a constant expenditure elasticity of approximately 0.625. Either assumption is a reasonable one, and each supports the conclusion that the real per capita consumption expenditures of peasants roughly doubled between 1978 and 1987.

An additional indicator of a rapid increase in the real incomes of peasants was the decline in the percentage of their food that was self-produced. In 1978 the peasants produced 76 percent of the food they consumed; nine years later this figure had fallen to 54 percent (SYOC 1988, 734). For all consumption, the percentage of self-produced food decreased from 60 percent to 36 percent. These changes were driven by two economic forces: increased real income, which made it possible to pay higher prices for products that had been processed to some degree, and an increased value of labor, which induced specialization in production, both in the enterprise or farm and the household.

### Urban Incomes and Consumption

The same sources used to determine peasant consumption and income were used to determine the increase in real urban consumption. The index of per capita consumption for nonagricultural residents increased by 76 percent between 1978 and 1987 (SYOC 1987, 711). This was an annual growth rate of 6.4 percent compared with a growth rate in the same series for peasants of 8.1 percent.

When the annual income available for living expenses—which is very similar to the series on consumption expenditures—was deflated by the index of the cost of living of staff and workers, the increase in the real disposable income of urban households was 86 percent. Although the two estimates are not the same, the difference is not large, and it might be reasonable to assume that the per capita consumption of urban households increased by roughly 80 percent and thus somewhat less than the increase in real consumption for rural households.

Urban food expenditures in 1978 accounted for 57.5 percent of total expenditures, according to the household survey for that year. From 1985 to 1987 the percentage allocated to food ranged from 52.2 percent to 53.5 percent. If the income elasticity of expenditure had been 0.7, an increase in real consumption of 80 percent would have reduced the portion spent on food to 50 percent, which is slightly lower than the actual percentage. Obviously, there can be several reasons for this discrepancy, including incorrect estimates of the expenditure elasticity for food and the increase in real income. But a more likely reason is that urban consumers spend a small fraction of their incomes on their highly subsidized housing. Consequently, even though urban consumers have much higher incomes than the peasants, urban consumers could have a higher elasticity of expenditure on food than peasants. If the urban income elasticity of demand had been 0.8, then an 80 percent increase in expenditure would have reduced the portion spent on food to 52.3 percent.

An important indicator of the increased consumption of urban households was the increased amount of living floor space, from 4.2 square meters in 1978 to 8.5 square meters in 1987 (SYOC 1988, 709). This increase cannot be used as a check on the increase in real incomes, however, because the increased space was not determined by each household allocating its income for this purpose. Rather, decisions about space were made by the political process. This process obviously recognized the improvement in income, but it is impossible to determine what particular income elasticity it may have used in arriving at the decision.

## Relative Incomes of Urban and Rural Families

There is perhaps no clearer indicator of the changes in rural and urban family incomes than that given in the following quotation from the August 25, 1989, issue of the *China Daily,* an English language newspaper published in China. The quotation is exact; it does not include a misprint: "In 1978, urban residents made almost two times more money than their rural neighbours did. The gap has decreased and now rural residents make nearly half as much as city dwellers." In other words, the outcome is ambiguous, and one has to wonder by what mysterious process the conclusion that "the gap has decreased. . . . " was arrived at.

In addition to the writer's failure to understand that "almost two times more money" is simply a reciprocal of "nearly half as much," the statement was factually incorrect about the income relationships in 1978. In 1978 per capita peasant incomes were 134 yuan, while the income available for living expenditures for staff and workers was 316 yuan. This is a ratio, not of almost 2:1 but of 2.35:1. I have included the quotation not to make fun, but to indicate how difficult it is to determine what changes, if any, have occurred in the relative incomes of rural and urban households in China.

The State Statistical Bureau publishes a comparison of consumption levels, measured in current prices, of peasants and nonagricultural residents. In 1978 the consumption of nonagricultural residents was 2.9 times that of peasants, declining to 2.3 times in 1983–1985, but increasing to 2.5 times in 1987 and probably somewhat beyond that in 1988. The table that includes these ratios carries the following interesting footnote: "Non-comparable factors of urban and rural prices are included" (SYOC 1988, 710). The noncomparable factors include urban families paying significantly lower prices for grain and vegetable oil than the prices used to value peasant consumption and the much lower housing costs of urban families.

Also according to the State Statistical Bureau, between 1978 and 1987 peasant consumption, measured in comparable prices, increased by 101 percent, while that of nonagricultural residents increased by 76 percent. By this measure of real consumption, there was some narrowing of the consumption gap between rural and urban areas. Data from the annual household surveys also indicate some narrowing; nevertheless, the gap remains large despite any narrowing that may have occurred. The result that in 1987 the ratio of the consumption level of nonagricultural residents to that of peasants was 2.5 (SYOC 1988, 710) is not likely to be an underestimate. Incidentally, the ratio of 2.5 for 1987 is the same as the average for 1952–1956; apparently, socialism has not had any significant effect on the relative income position of the peasants in more than three decades, in spite of all claims that Chinese socialism not only gave a high value to egalitarianism but actually did something about it. As far as rural-urban income inequality is concerned, there has been no reduction.

The great difference in rural and urban housing costs illustrates some of the difficulties in comparing rural and urban consumption levels by the usual measures. In 1987 urban families spent 2.2 percent of their consumption expenditures on rent, water, electricity, and gas, and an additional 3.9 percent on house and construction materials and fuel, for a total of 6.1 percent of expenditures devoted to housing. Rural families allocated 14.5 percent to housing and 4.8 percent to fuel, for a total of 19.3 percent. Out of total expenditures on consumption that were less than half those of urban households, peasant families spent 75 yuan per capita on housing in 1987, while urban families spent just 54 yuan. Although it is true that rural people had almost twice as much housing space in 1987 as did urban families—16.0 square meters compared with 8.5 square meters—rural people paid the full cost of their housing, while the urban population paid only a small fraction of their housing cost.

Some idea of the magnitude of the Chinese government's bias against peasants is given by a comparison of the state's investment in urban housing from 1980 to 1987—121 billion yuan—with the state's investment in agriculture—30 billion yuan (SYOC 1988, 503 and 505). This disproportion existed even though 74 percent of the labor force in 1987 was classified as "collective and individual labourers in rural areas" (SYOC 1988, 123) for whose housing the state takes no responsibility whatsoever.

## Reform and Income Inequality

One of the objections to economic reform in the centrally planned economies is the significant increase in income inequality that may result. Often such objections seem based on the assumption that at a given time the socialist system had achieved a high degree of income equality. The previous section made it clear that the socialist system in China did not achieve income equality between urban and rural areas, since urban per capita consumption was estimated to be 2.9 times rural per capita consumption in 1978, the year before the initiation of the rural reforms.

As noted in the previous section, there may have been some small diminution in the discrepancy between urban and rural consumption levels under the reforms; however, the general impression among Chinese scholars is that the reforms have increased income inequality. The evidence on changes in income distribution is limited. An analysis based on the annual household consumption surveys compared a measure of the inequality of the income distribution—the Gini coefficient—for 1978 and 1984 (*Beijing Review,* 1985, no. 29). It indicated that income inequality had increased in rural areas, from 0.237 in 1978 to 0.264 in 1984, and decreased somewhat in urban areas, from 0.185 in 1978 to 0.168 in 1984 (*Beijing Review,* 1985, no. 29, 22). The increase in rural areas should have been expected; in fact, one of the intended results of the reforms was to relate reward more closely to productivity. Such a result would inevitably lead to an increase in inequality within communities in the short run and perhaps in the longer run as well. The coefficient for rural areas in 1984 still implies a relatively high degree of income equality, since agricultural incomes vary significantly from year to year because of natural factors such as weather, diseases, and insects. The urban coefficients are not too surprising, since the urban and industrial reforms did little to change the structure of compensation.

Changes in the distribution of income among geographic areas are more relevant to understanding the effects of the reforms on income distribution than are changes in the personal distribution of income. Given the nature of the rural reforms, a significant increase in the inequality of provincial average incomes of the rural population would have been expected. As noted in Chapter 3, the relative importance of nonagricultural incomes has increased significantly since 1978, when they accounted for 7 percent of peasant family incomes; by 1987 this portion had increased to 25.4 percent.

The rural areas near urban centers have the greatest potential for increasing incomes from nonagricultural sources. Because earnings from nonagricultural employment have been significantly greater than earnings from agricultural employment during the reform period, it is reasonable to expect that the rural areas in coastal regions or near large cities such as Beijing would gain in income relative to the less well-situated areas in the interior of the country. In 1986, for example, 30.6 percent of the income of all rural residents came from enterprises in townships and villages. In the Beijing municipality, however, 56.7 percent of incomes came from this source; in Jiangsu (near Shanghai), 52.8 percent; and in Liaoning, 4.8 percent. But in the provinces of Inner Mongolia, Guangxi, Guizhou, Xinjiang, and Yunnan, all located in the interior, none received more than 16 percent of their incomes from such enterprises (CAY 1987, 289).

Surprisingly, there has not been a sharp widening of provincial income differentials. In fact, there has been little widening, if any. For five of the ten interior or western provinces for which the per capita incomes of rural residents have been given for 1978, there was some widening of the income differences between 1978 and 1987 (SYOC 1988, 736). Four provinces, however, had income increases greater than the national average, while five had smaller increases and one had the same increase. For this approach to provincial income differentials, a difference in income growth of 5 percent was assumed to be within the margin of error relative to the national average or random variation. Thus, differences had to be greater than 5 percent to be counted as plus or minus.

Another approach is to compare the unweighted average of the per capita incomes of rural households with the average of per capita incomes nationally. In 1978 the unweighted average of the per capita incomes of peasant households of the ten interior provinces was 83 percent of the national average. The first effect of the reforms, due primarily to the price increases, was to increase the incomes in the ten provinces to 91 percent of the national average. By 1984 the relative income had declined to 88 percent and then to 85 percent in 1987 (SYOC 1988, 736). But even with the decline in the comparative income position between 1980 and 1987, the 1987 average incomes of rural households in the ten interior provinces were slightly higher relative to the national average than in 1978.

The data available on incomes in sixteen interior provinces for 1980, 1984, 1985, and 1987 reveal that in 1980 their average per capita rural income was 86 percent of the national average, increasing to 88 percent in 1984 and to 90 percent in 1985, and declining to 85 percent in 1987. If the six additional provinces are considered separately, their unweighted average per capita income was only 76 percent of the national per capita income in 1980, increasing to 89 percent in 1984, and declining to 84 percent in 1987.

These results are consistent with the view that there has been little widening of the provincial income differences. The trend in the relative incomes in recent years, however, could support the view that the provincial income differentials will widen in the years ahead.

Some insight into the effects of reforms on provincial income differences may be gained by reviewing the experience of four well-situated farm areas. These provinces or municipalities, which are on the coast (or near it), have major cities as their core economic units. In 1986 in Beijing, Shanghai, Tianjin, and Jiangsu, income from township and village enterprises accounted for more than 50 percent of the net incomes of rural families compared with a national average of 31 percent and generally 20 percent or less for the interior provinces (CAY

1987, 289). The favorably situated geographic areas had the least to gain from the increase in prices of farm products and the most to gain from the expansion of employment in industry, construction, transportation, and marketing.

It appears that this is generally what happened. From 1978 to 1980, the period most affected by the increased procurement prices, rural incomes in both Beijing and Shanghai fell relative to the national average. Jiangsu showed no change in its relative income position, and Tianjin showed a small increase. But from 1980 to 1984 or to 1987, there was a consistent increase in each of the four areas in the ratio of their average incomes to the national average. The increase in relative income was greatest for Beijing: from 150 percent of the national average in 1980 to 198 percent in 1987. The increase for Shanghai was from 208 percent in 1980 to 229 percent in 1987, and Tianjin and Jiangsu showed significant increases as well.

The reforms instituted in 1979 and subsequent years resulted in substantial increases in the real incomes and consumption levels of both rural and urban households. While it is difficult to determine exactly how large the increases were, a substantial body of evidence indicates a rough doubling of the real consumption level of peasants and a minimum increase of 80 percent for urban households. Apparently, however, the available official data on consumption of urban households does not accurately reflect the substantial increase in the amount and quality of housing nor the large increase in various forms of in-kind subsidies provided to the urban population. Consequently, the per capita real consumption of urban households probably increased by more than 80 percent.

There is little evidence that the large gap in real incomes between the countryside and the city has been narrowed, either during the reform period or during the longer period of socialized agriculture. The tight control over migration from country to city has prevented an important equilibratory mechanism. Most of the shift of labor out of agriculture has stemmed from the development of nonagricultural activities in rural areas. While this development has occurred at a remarkable rate since the early 1980s, it has only been sufficient to prevent the income gap from widening.

## CHAPTER 6

# Failure of Macroeconomic Policies

The failure of the Chinese authorities to achieve effective control of credit and the money supply has imposed enormous costs on the Chinese people and has done great harm to the process of economic reform. It is not too far-fetched to place some of the responsibility for the events of May and June 1989 on the failure to control inflation. A considerable part of the justifiable concern over corruption was caused by the failure of the government to hold inflation in check and to carry out price reform. The students attracted supporters for their demonstrations from those whose salaries were frozen or very sticky and who were faced with significant losses of real income as prices increased by a fourth in a year.

### Why Loss of Macroeconomic Control?

Loss of control over the macroeconomics of the system is especially difficult to comprehend given the history of modern China, the effective control of money and credit for most of the period of communism, and the ideological neutrality of maintaining a stable price level. But however difficult it is to comprehend why it happened, there can be no doubt about the adverse consequences. This section draws heavily on an article entitled "Seriously Sum up the Experiences of 10 Years of Reform" published by Xue Muqiao in late 1988 (FBIS-CHI-89-003, January 5, 1989). Some might consider the article mistitled. Rather than summarizing and emphasizing the positive outcomes of the reforms, it deals primarily with the loss of macroeconomic control of the economy and the need to return to the path of extending the role of the market.

According to Xue, the reforms moved successfully along the desired path for the first five years, through 1983. As evidence of the successes he noted that

> we reasonably readjusted the proportions of agriculture, light industry and heavy industry and basically established a proper ratio between the accumulation of funds and consumption. We also improved the supply of the means of production to a certain extent and produced a relatively adequate supply of consumer goods. As a result, the buyers were in a more favorable position in the market of some commodities. (18–19)

After noting the progress made during the previous five years, the Third Plenary Session of the Twelfth CPC Central Committee in 1984 called for an "all-round reform of the economic structure" with the aim of creating "a socialist commodity economy." Thus, the law of value and the principle of commodity exchange would guide the economy; it would not be a planned production economy. The latter is an economy in which the decisions are highly centralized, as had been the case in China for the previous three decades. The reform of the price system was "the key to reform of the entire economic structure."

Xue rationalized what occurred:

> According to the new guiding ideology, we should have a firm grip on macroeconomic control and adopt a loose and liberal control over microeconomic activities in our economic management. However, owing to our lack of experience in macro-control under the conditions of commodity economy, especially the experience in utilizing the wonderful tool of banking mechanism, a situation has emerged since the 4th quarter of 1984 in which bank credit has been out of control, investments are "overheated," the scale of capital construction has been too large and the money supply has been too great. (19)

He continued by noting that the growth of industrial production in 1985 and subsequent years had been too rapid and that prices had increased by a "great margin," which induced the government to set price limits on many commodities, including commodities that previously had been freed of price controls and for which market forces had determined the prices. He also noted that with the reimposition of price controls, the opportunities for corruption were increased when "many government organizations and businessmen took advantage of the great difference between controlled price and market price and bought commodities for reselling at a huge profit."

Investment in fixed assets in all sectors of the economy and by all economic units was 96 billion yuan in 1981. This increased to 143 billion yuan in 1983 and then really took off, more than doubling by 1986 when it was 301 billion yuan with a further increase to 364 billion yuan in 1987 (SYOC 1988, 493). Between 1978 and 1983 the amount of money in circulation increased by 150 percent, while the gross output value of agriculture and industry increased by 63 percent. Xue estimated that between 1983 and 1988 the money supply increased by 250–300 percent, much faster than the increase in real output. The obvious and inevitable consequence was inflation.

Table 7 shows the price indexes for 1978 to mid-1989. The indexes indicate that for 1979–1984, except for 1980, increases in the cost-of-living indexes and price indexes were modest—generally 3 percent or less. In 1985, however, the increases grew, culminating in large increases in 1988 and the first half of 1989. The cost of living of urban workers increased by 21 percent in 1988 and by a further 18 percent during the first half of 1989 relative to 1988.

## Decentralization: Not Always the Way to Go

An important objective of the reforms of 1978 and 1984 was to decentralize many economic decisions, either by delegating decisions that were formerly made in Beijing to provincial and municipal authorities or by permitting enterprises to respond to market forces. In agriculture the decentralization of a large number of decisions to local authorities and individual households had worked very well, and apparently this success influenced decisions made in 1984 on urban and industrial reforms.

For decentralization of decisions to result in greater efficiency of production and resource allocation, the decision-making units must

TABLE 7 Indexes of Retail Prices, Cost of Living, and Purchase Prices of Farm Products, 1978–1989

| Year | Retail prices[a] | Cost of living[b] | Purchase prices of farm products[c] |
|---|---|---|---|
| 1978 | 100 | 100 | 100 |
| 1979 | 102 | 102 | 122 |
| 1980 | 108 | 110 | 131 |
| 1981 | 111 | 112 | 139 |
| 1982 | 113 | 115 | 142 |
| 1983 | 114 | 117 | 148 |
| 1984 | 118 | 120 | 154 |
| 1985 | 128 | 134 | 167 |
| 1986 | 136 | 144 | 178 |
| 1987 | 146 | 156 | 199 |
| 1988 | 173 | 185 | n.a. |
| 1989 | 204[d] | 215[e] | n.a. |

n.a. = not available.
a. Includes list prices, negotiated prices, and market prices.
b. Index is for urban staff and workers.
c. Includes list prices, negotiated prices, prices for above-quota purchases, and contrast prices.
d. In June 1989 the retail price index was 23 percent above June 1988.
e. In June 1989 the cost of living index was 22 percent above June 1988.
SOURCE: *China Statistical Yearbook,* 1988, 691, and *Beijing Review* 33 (9): v.

have the appropriate signals to which to respond. If the signals are inappropriate—if the prices are badly amiss, for example—production decisions can result in many products being produced in excess quantities, while other products may not be produced at all or produced in far too small amounts. Excess production is possible for state enterprises in China because the state marketing agency is committed to accepting all planned output at the fixed price. Thus, it may be some years before a limit is placed on the outputs that are in excess of the amounts demanded. When there is significant inflationary pressure, the primary loss of efficiency will be due to the production of inadequate amounts of products with low fixed prices; many of the products with high fixed prices will be bought simply because they are all that are available. Based on personal observation in May 1989 in the

Soviet Union and in August 1989 in China, however, the availability of goods in retail stores has been much more adversely affected in the Soviet Union than in China. The prices of consumer goods have been significantly more flexible in China than in the Soviet Union.

Before 1978 control of credit and the money supply was relatively simple because all capital construction by state enterprises was financed by state appropriations, and there was strict control over wage rates. Any investment beyond that undertaken by state enterprises was relatively limited, and a significant share of the investment undertaken by rural communes was limited by the quantities of machinery, equipment, and materials available. After 1979 the state appropriations were gradually replaced by funds at the disposal of local governments and enterprises from retained profits or taxes collected by the local governments, and by bank loans. There was no satisfactory mechanism for limiting the total value of bank loans.

Before mid-1984 the banks were still very much an integral part of the central government of China. According to Xue, until then the banks were following that old Chinese practice of "everyone eating from the same big pot." The banks turned over their deposits to the states and, in turn, requested loans from the state. Over the next two years there was a reform in which the banks, largely at the provincial level, made loans on the basis of their own deposits and were permitted to make their own management decisions.

The system apparently got off to a bad start because of an announcement made in October 1984—in response to the rapid expansion of credit in that year—that the ceiling for loans in 1985 would be the actual level of loans issued in 1984. The announcement must have been made too early, for as Xue noted, "there were serious imbalances in the credit submitted by the banks in the fourth quarter of 1984" (21). Obviously, the 1984 loan volumes were inflated by the increasing demand for loans during the last quarter.

But the weakness in the control of credit and money supply did not end with the reforms instituted in 1984. The banks, including the People's Bank of China, remained subject to a significant degree of political influence and control. In fact, an independent central bank does not yet exist in China. Xue described the situation that confronted the banks from 1985 until at least late 1988:

> Due to lingering administrative interference in bank loans, the banks were unable to turn down requests for loans by various provinces, cities, and counties for carrying out huge construction projects. There

> were numerous "projects approved by leading cadres" and "projects approved with leader's notes." Even without funds at its disposal, a company, once approved by higher authorities, could rely on bank loans for its operations. Thousands of privileged companies were set up in recent years with the approval of leading cadres at different levels. (21)

Xue also wrote that as of the end of 1988 banks still did not have the full authority to set a national credit limit and stick to it.

Outstanding bank loans at the end of 1987 stood at 903 billion yuan, almost double the comparable figure of approximately 480 billion yuan at the end of 1984.[4] The decisions made in late 1984 did not slow the growth of credit; the growth accelerated. The volume of loans increased by approximately 88 percent in the three-year period from 1985 to 1987 compared with 60 percent for the three years ending with 1984.

Xue agreed that it was necessary to slow down the pace of price reform for the next two years. But he hastened to add:

> This, however, cannot be construed to mean that we want to give up the price reform. On the contrary, the purpose of our efforts to improve the economic environment is to check inflation and pave the way for the price reform. This must be understood by everyone. If we do not reform our price system, we cannot establish the new order of the socialist commodity economy, and if we fail to check inflation, our price reform will be out of the question. (22)

One can only hope that after the events of June 1989 and with the apparent change in the locus of power in the Communist party that it is "understood by everyone" that price reform is essential for the continued vitality of the Chinese economy.

It must be emphasized, however, that there may be an ominous side of the efforts to limit the extension of credit, especially for construction but with obvious spillovers to credit for current enterprise operations. The guidelines to the credit-tightening policy have been stated in terms of "three guarantees and three restrictions." The three guarantees for financing construction and investment apply to projects in the state plan, productive projects, and essential state projects. The three restrictions apply to projects that are outside the state plan, nonproductive projects, and nonessential projects. Undoubtedly, this credit policy will further entrench the large state enterprises, will cause a retrenchment in small and other collective enterprises in the cities, and will adversely affect all rural enterprises, whether they are operated by townships, villages, or private individuals.

Such effects are justified, even by Xue, on the grounds that many of the rural industries produce products of poor quality and utilize energy and raw materials inefficiently. I have seen no evidence to back up such assertions, although casual observations indicate that by some standards the output of many rural factories is low in quality. The same can be said, however, about the output of state enterprises. An important observation here—and one seemingly ignored even by someone as astute and well informed as Xue—is that if a rural collective or private enterprise produces a product of such poor quality that buyers cannot be found, it will go broke and cease producing such products. But state enterprises are not faced with this alternative; no matter how poor the quality of their output, such enterprises are not forced into bankruptcy. The credit policy and other policies dealing with the allocation of raw materials are basically designed to protect the monopoly position of the large state enterprises against the upstart enterprises in rural areas. Consequently, the brunt of the adverse effects of the deflationary policies instituted in late 1988 will fall on rural enterprises and rural people. This outcome, of course, is consistent with the urban bias discussed in Chapter 1.

## High Investment and Accumulation Rates

The Chinese economy seems to have an inherent tendency to let the rate of investment or accumulation get out of control. It is agreed by economists in China that the share of accumulation in national income in 1978 and 1979 was excessive at about 35 percent. The rate was lowered to less than 29 percent in 1981 and 1982, but in 1985–1987 it once again rose to an average of nearly 35 percent. The decentralization of decision making to local governments and enterprises is one of the reasons for the surge in investment, but it is not the sole or even the primary culprit in the surge of investment. At least two other economic factors are of much greater significance.

One of these economic factors is the very small real net cost of funds borrowed by an enterprise to make an investment. Under current regulations borrowed funds are repaid with pretax funds. If the tax rate is 50–70 percent of profits, half or more of the cost of the investment is borne by the government and not by the enterprise. A related economic factor is the very low interest rates in nominal terms. When the rate of inflation has been 20 percent or more, the real rate of interest has been negative, perhaps as low as minus 15 percent. Consequently, when these two factors are taken into account, the net cost of borrowed funds to the enterprise may be nil.

Actually, the incentives to investment may be even more bizarre than has been indicated so far. Provincial and local governments have an interest in expanding economic activity in their areas because it is from taxes on these activities that they obtain a considerable fraction of their revenues. Xue acknowledged this difficulty when he noted that local governments were acquiring more of their investment funds from credit than from direct appropriations from the state. He described the outcome of making the local governments and enterprises responsible for their finances as introducing the practice of "everyone eating from one's own pot." This, of course, contrasts with "everyone eating from the same big pot," but it has its adverse consequences as well. Because local governments must obtain a significant share of their revenues from local sources, it is in their interest to encourage local industrial development, and especially so if the investment is based on borrowed funds at low interest rates and with repayment from pretax profits, thereby reducing the taxes paid to the central government. Because the local governments obtain their revenues from product taxes, they are not adversely affected by a loss of revenue to the central government.

These observations clearly support the view that when there are numerous distortions in the economy, partial reforms often create as many, if not more, problems than they solve. The significant distortions in this instance are the negative real interest rates and the right to repay bank loans with pretax income, two conditions that make borrowed funds available at little real cost. Consequently, the rush to expand investment and construction by enterprises and local governments is fully understandable. What is not understandable is why the central government does not change the rules of the game to require that all loans be repaid in after-tax dollars and to charge a positive real rate of interest. Obviously, there are many other distortions, including those of input and output prices. But even if input and output prices were not distorted, the present terms for acquiring and repaying loans would result in excessive and inappropriate investments.

## Budget Deficits

It was not only the credit policy, or lack of one, that led to the inflationary situation after 1985; the modest budget deficit of 1985 grew rapidly in the succeeding three years. The official estimate of the budget balance in 1985 was a small surplus of 2.2 billion yuan (SYOC 1988, 665). This surplus, however, included 9 billion yuan in borrowed funds, so that by more conventional accounting there was a deficit of 6.8 billion yuan or roughly 3 percent of total governmental expenditures. In 1986 and 1987 the budget deficit, including loans, increased to 20.9 billion yuan and 24.6 billion yuan, respectively, or roughly 10 percent of expenditures. In 1988 the deficit increased to 34 billion yuan or 13 percent of expenditures.

The deficits were primarily financed by the conventional means, the issuance of money. While some of the deficit was covered by the issuance of bonds that were purchased by the public, most of the borrowing was from the banks. Consequently, the deficit was translated rather quickly into an increase in the money supply.

**Causes of the deficit.** The obvious cause of the budget deficit was that the government spent more than it received in taxes and other current receipts. Three categories of expenditure increases are worth noting, however: two forms of direct expenditure—for price subsidies and construction—and one form of expenditure that affected both expenditures and revenues—the wage bill in state enterprises.

In 1988 direct consumer price subsidies amounted to 31.7 billion yuan. These subsidies reduce the prices of grain and vegetable oil paid by urban consumers and cover the losses incurred in importing five commodities. But this is only part of the subsidy bill that is associated directly with urban consumption. On different occasions when price ceilings were lifted on important food products such as pork and vegetables, per capita subsidies were introduced to cover the anticipated increase in consumer expenditures stemming from the price increases.

It is not clear how much of the total subsidy bill for urban consumers is related to food price policy. One article stated that in 1988 the subsidy cost was 29 percent of the "national revenue and expenditure" (FBIS-CHI-89-139, July 21, 1989, 32). It is assumed that the reference is to government expenditure. If so, and if nearly all of the subsidies are either direct price subsidies on food or income supplements to compensate for increased food prices, the food subsidy bill in 1988 was in the range of 75 billion to 80 billion yuan. Although the article referred to a wide variety of subsidies—for example the one-child, schooling, transportation, hair-cutting, and funeral subsidies—it noted: "Most of the subsidy usually goes for grain" (32).

The government assumed some responsibility for fueling the increase in expenditures when it sharply increased the appropriations for capital construction for 1986–1988 (64 billion yuan) to about double the average for 1981–1982 (32 billion yuan)—these amounts, which are included in the government budget, are about a fifth of total construction expenditures. Thus doubling in nominal terms is substantially greater than the increase in the general price level.

One consequence of decentralization has been a reduction in central control over wages. Given the approaches used to collect government revenue from state enterprises, the wage bill becomes a competitor with revenue. Substantial increases in wages and bonuses act to reduce government revenue, even under the enterprise responsibility contracts. It is clearly more in the short-run interest of enterprise managers to pay higher wages and bonuses than to pay more taxes to the government. In 1988 total wages paid increased by 21.2 percent and bonuses increased much more, by 44.6 percent (FBIS-CHI-89-066, April 7, 1989, 38).

**Consequences for reform.** The effort to bring inflation under control has significant negative ramifications for continuing or even maintaining the reforms in rural and urban areas. By mid-1989 it was clear that there had been a significant detour along the road to reform; price controls were reinstituted on several food products that had been freed of control, and rural markets for some farm products were being limited or in some cases closed. These changes have already been announced for cotton and probably also apply to soybeans and other sources of vegetable oils, silkworms, and generally products that are raw materials for subsequent processing.

## CHAPTER 7

# Rural Reforms: Unfinished Business

Although the achievements of rural reforms must be admired, recent policy errors are causing many to lose confidence in the reforms. This loss of confidence is evidenced by the reimposition of price controls, restraints on the freedom to utilize markets for farm products, and the failure to proceed with price reform generally.

The rural reforms were quite remarkable in terms of their scope and effectiveness. Nevertheless, a number of important issues were left unresolved, and some remain unresolved a decade later—important unfinished business. Unfortunately, the turmoil and struggle of 1989 make it unlikely that these important issues will be faced until well into the 1990s, if at all.

### Ownership of Land

A lack of clarity remains about the ownership of farmland. If one asks in China who owns farmland, one of two answers is likely to be forthcoming: the state or the collective. The first is incorrect de jure but may often be correct de facto. The correct answer, according to the constitution of China, is that almost all farmland is owned by collectives. The minor exception is that portion of agricultural land in the state farms.

Communes were organized in a three-tier system, consisting of the commune, the brigade, and the production team. The ownership of the land was supposed to rest with the production teams. When the production team was the basic accounting unit of the commune, ownership of the land by the team had very important implications for the distribution of income within the brigade and the commune. But when either the commune, as in the case of Dazhai, or the brigade was the basic accounting unit and determined the distribution of income, the production team's role as legal owner of the land was of little importance. Such ownership did not protect their rights to the income from their land and other assets. Because the ownership of the land by the production team has been violated with considerable frequency in the past and with the approval of the highest political authority, it is very important that the land ownership issue be settled unambiguously and soon.

If one asks which collective owns the land, the likely response will be the village. But village has two different meanings: natural villages and administrative villages. The natural villages are simply families living together in a specific area. The administrative village consists of a production team, and because natural villages have been physically rebuilt in the recent rural housing boom, the families may not live contiguously.

Although there is undoubtedly variation from area to area in China, in some villages that I visited the true control of farmland appears to rest with the natural village even when formerly it had several production teams. Since the original allocation of land to the production teams had a considerable element of historical arbitrariness and resulted in considerable income inequality within a natural village where there were several production teams, the treatment of a natural village as a unit in terms of allocating land resources is not without some merit. As the ownership of land is shifted from teams to villages, however, the uncertainty over the ownership of land is increased.

The township is also a collective unit, and it is clear that in some cases the township has emerged as the real owner of the land (see Chapter 8). Thus, further uncertainty has been created.

**Security of Rights to Use Land**

In a report on a seminar held in Guizhou Province in the summer of 1988 it was stated:

> The stipulation on ownership is fuzzy and the contents of and the line of demarcation between collective ownership and land use rights of farming households are also unclear. . . . What with the lack of continuity and system in the land policy and the lack of legal and institutional protection for land ownership violation of rights occur frequently. An investigation carried out in the land system reform experimental zone in Guizhou's Meitan County shows that 90 percent of the civil disputes in the county have to do with the lack of distinction of land ownership. (FBIS-CHI-88-251, December 30, 1988, 43)

The lack of clarity over the ownership of land or the lack of an institution to enforce the ownership of land means that the assignment of rights to use the land to individual households has a considerable degree of insecurity. The national policy, as stated in 1984, is that the rights to use land are to be assigned for fifteen years; this followed a trial period in which the rights generally had been assigned for three years (Du 1989, 82). In none of the villages that I have visited, however, have the land rights been assigned for more than three years, although, according to a knowledgeable informant, in many areas of China assignments have been made for periods longer than three years.

The security of land-use rights is important because of its effect on the willingness of farmers to invest in both maintaining and improving the land. The issue goes beyond a given family's right to use land in its village to whether that right exists for an extended period of time for particular pieces of land. Land has been allocated among households on an egalitarian basis. In some villages the sole criterion has been the number of members of the household—a family of six would receive 50 percent more land than a family of four. In other villages the land might be divided into two components: a food plot and a responsibility plot. Food plots, formed by dividing a certain share of land in the village on a per capita basis, carry with them no obligation to deliver grain to the state. Villagers with responsibility plots—land divided among the households on the basis of number of workers—must make deliveries to the state, however.

Assuming that one of the two systems is ultimately adopted, why is there a problem of security of the land-use rights? It arises because many, if not most, villages reallocate the land as household sizes change over time from births, deaths, and marriages. Such redistributions may occur annually or every two or three years. But even if a household's share of the land in the village remains unchanged, the household cannot be sure that it will be reassigned the same land that it had been farming. Consequently, long-term investment in improving the land is discouraged.

In a thoughtful and perceptive article entitled "Land System: Valid Property Rights, Long-Term Tenancy, and Paid Transfer" (FBIS-CHI-88-226, November 23, 1988), Zhou Qiren made the exceedingly important point that the land system was a property rights system and that the fundamental point of any such system was *the validity of property rights*. He also pointed out that a variety of land systems were possible and that many well-functioning ones were found in the world. What differentiates an efficient land system from others, he observed, is the validity and clarity of property rights. According to Zhou, property rights have three main economic functions. First, property rights define who has the rights to obtain income and to allocate resources. With well-defined property rights, no individual, family, or enterprise can take the returns or the resources away from any other individual, family, or enterprise who has ownership of the property rights. Second, property rights encourage people to utilize their labor in association with the resource designated in the property right. People are motivated in this way because they "can thus have a stable anticipation of the results of labor input." And third, valid property rights encourage investment. Finally, Zhou made the striking point that "when property rights are not clearly defined, and when the role of property rights cannot be brought into full play, other substitutes can be used. One substitute is coercion, using political power to get compulsory input, accumulation, and change" (42).

It is not possible to do full justice to Zhou's article, which made a convincing case for the transferability of contract rights to land, including permanent tenancy, subject to certain constraints such as not permitting division of the property right among several children. He did not argue for the private ownership of land; it would still be collectively owned. But he wisely argued that the present understanding of what collective ownership means in China did not adequately provide for a valid and enforceable property rights system.

Zhou has accepted the view that the departure point for a land system in China is the notion that land is under the collective ownership of peasants: "The question is: To which collective level does this collective belong? The system foundation descended from the commune is: 'Three-level system of ownership, with the team as the basic unit.' The meaning of this foundation itself is vague. Such a vague real estate main body cannot establish the foundation for a land system in China" (43). According to Zhou, the production teams should be considered the collective unit that owns the land. Of the several reasons given for this conclusion, one was quite pragmatic: the most accurate information about the historical changes in the land system is in the records of the production teams. He noted the absence of documents or materials about changes in land control from the period between the land reform of the early 1950s and the introduction of the household responsibility system. Other reasons included the knowledge possessed by production team members about the land and its attributes; production teams are thus in the best position to resist administrative intervention.

Zhou made a strong case that the Chinese government should allocate ownership of land to the production teams and that allocation should be followed by establishment of the appropriate records to define clearly where the property right resides. This is the only way that local authorities can be prevented from infringing on the property right of the teams.

James Wen (1989) has shown both analytically and empirically that the insecurity of land-use rights has inhibited investment in land improvements. For example, one reason the quality and productivity of farmland has been maintained after centuries of intensive cultivation is the application of organic fertilizers to the land. The returns on the labor-intensive application of such fertilizers, which include both animal manures and night soil, occur over a period of years and over a longer period than is the case with chemical fertilizers. The combined effects of the increased value of time since 1978 and the insecurity of the rights to use land have resulted in a reduction in the application of such fertilizers with some possible long-run adverse effects on land productivity.

Wen also attributed some part of the large investment in rural housing to the insecurity of land-use rights. Under Communist rule, and since the establishment of socialized agriculture, the property right to one's house has not been challenged. Thus, an investment in housing is considered to be secure—it will not be expropriated, it can be passed on to the next generation, and it can be sold. Because investment in land improvement is not nearly as secure, investment in housing receives preference.

In spite of the problems created by the insecurity of land-use rights, there has not been a concerted effort to resolve the problem. The reasons for not making progress in this area include the ideological and the political. An ideological reason is that if and when land rights are fully secured, there will be pressure for the right to either rent or sell the use rights and perhaps the land itself. The current national policy permits the transfer of land contracts, but it is hedged with restrictions that reveal the ideological bias against the operation of markets that exist in many quarters. In their discussion of the household contracting of land Lou Yousheng and Gao Kuanzhong noted:

> The principle of freedom to contract is of great significance to the opening up of a land contract rights market. For example, in setting the price of the contract rights transfer, present policies forbid "undeserved profit from the transfer of contracts." . . . It is very difficult for the government to stipulate a rational and legitimate profit, the price of contract rights transfer differs with time, place, and people. The price should be negotiated and set by the two parties involved. The prohibition against "undeserved profit" often obstructs the necessary and rational flow of land. (FBIS-CHI-89-011, January 18, 1989, 37)

This stipulation clearly means that authorities become directly involved in all land transfers and thus seriously inhibit the creation of an active and effective functioning market in land-use rights.

The political reason for not setting clearly and unambiguously the rights to use land is that any such step would reduce the power of local authorities: the village head, the secretaries of the Communist party at the county, township, and village levels, and other local authorities. When circumstances are ambiguous, as they now are with land-use rights, a considerable range exists for the arbitrary use of power. Local authorities would lose a great deal of discretionary authority, however, if they were not permitted to reassign land-use rights because those rights could be voluntarily transferred only by the household owner.

Thus, in view of the ideological objections to private property rights in means of production and the resistance of powerful local authorities, it is perhaps not too surprising that a decade has not been long enough to settle this important issue. One of the consequences of this failure is the rising tide of views that the rural reforms are no longer appropriate and that new forms of management and contractual arrangements are required. Chapter 8 presents some evidence that these views represent a real threat to the continued existence of the household responsibility system.

## Incomplete Transfer of the Governmental Functions of Communes

When the communes were abolished, generally in 1983 and 1984, some of the governmental functions performed by the communes were not transferred to local government units. The nonagricultural enterprises were transferred to township organizations called (approximately) agricultural, industrial, and commercial corporations, and, at least in some cases, the running of these corporations seemed to be the primary role accepted by the townships. The governmental functions were transferred to county, township, and village governments, though apparently with little explanation and few guidelines. Nor was there much effort to educate the peasants about the reality of what had happened under the commune system. The peasants resisted the taxes levied by local governments to cover government activities such as schools, health clinics, public security, and roads, even though they had paid for such functions under the commune system through the costs of the activities being subtracted from commune income before its distribution to the members.

One of the most serious items of unfinished business was the failure to provide governmental institutions to manage certain types of infrastructure, especially water projects. If a water project includes an area entirely within the boundaries of a given governmental unit such as a county or township, it is well within the capacity of such units to manage the project. But medium- and large-scale projects often cut across the boundaries of the responsible governmental units. In such cases, most governments have created special management units that have limited governmental powers such as the right to charge fees for services received, the right to allocate the services among the recipients, and the right to spend the funds to maintain and improve facilities.

Reportedly, some of the irrigation facilities in China have not been maintained and operated appropriately since the introduction of the household responsibility system. There could be three reasons for this. First, the central government has greatly reduced the real value of funds allocated to rural water projects. Second, the appropriate institutional arrangements have not been created to provide for the maintenance of the water projects. And third, some of the projects may not have been worth maintaining because the returns were not sufficient to cover the costs.

The third reason was hinted at by my hero of the rural reforms, Du Runsheng, in his response to a question about whether it was true that development of China's irrigation system at basic levels had been weakened by reduced investment, and, if so, whether there was any way to solve the problem. Du answered:

> Investments have dropped, but the system's efficiency has increased. Most water conservancy projects were built in a short time and on a large scale. Therefore, they are in a poor condition and some of them are not complete systems. Now we are starting to consolidate achievements, completing them into systems and improving their quality. In some areas, irrigation systems are really weakened; however, the peasants won't easily give up on water conservancy and existing problems will certainly be resolved. (Du 1989, 189)

Thus, the third reason is that there may have been irrigation systems so poorly planned and constructed that they were not worth maintaining and preserving.

In any case, the blame for any negligence in maintaining irrigation systems should be placed on the failure to create appropriate institutional arrangements and not on the responsibility system. Private individuals with no governmental authority cannot be expected to provide public goods. Only when individuals are legally permitted to organize and to require payment for the services rendered can they undertake the provision of services that are made available to others.

## Incomplete Price Reform

Although there are several reasons for the success of the rural reforms, two factors related to prices and markets merit considerable importance: (1) a relative price structure within agriculture that was not far out of balance in 1978, and (2) the expansion of existing markets and the opening of new markets for agricultural products in both rural and urban areas. These factors, combined with the removal of the restraints on nonfarm activities and the introduction of the household responsibility system, go a considerable distance in explaining the success achieved.

But, as the reforms have succeeded, agricultural output has increased, and agriculture's dependence on purchased inputs has increased, the failure to achieve a significant reform of the industrial price structure has imposed substantial costs on agriculture. The combination of quota and above-quota prices for grains and other farm products before 1985 and the contract prices, which were not drastically below the market prices for most farm products until 1987, provided reasonable incentives for farm production. With inflation and the rapid growth in demand for most farm products, however, the increases in contract purchase prices have been insufficient to keep up with the market prices since 1986.

An article on the difficulties of paying for the procurements of grain and oilseeds reported that as of May 1989 the market price of grain was three times the contract purchase price (FBIS-CHI-89-093 May 16, 1989, 70). This implies that the contract purchase prices no longer are effective guides to the allocation of agricultural resources. Thus, the production, or at least the marketing, of grain has become a forced, not a voluntary transaction.

According to Liu Zifu and Wang Man, a significant share of the 1988 grain procurements was obtained by force or exercise of monopoly power (FBIS-CHI-89-072, April 17, 1989, 58–61). For example: "According to some county level cadres in Anhui, Jiangxi, Jiangsu, and Hunan, around 70 percent of the public grain was gathered by the county and township cadres from the peasants' homes by force" (59). They then added that

> some localities played the card of family planning while collecting grain. If a young couple want to give birth to a child, they had to deliver grain first. Otherwise, their child would not be registered, or they would be fined. Regarding the households which could not fulfill the quotas, their children were not allowed to go to school. . . . Regarding the households which refused to deliver or delivered less grain, a number of localities took their cash, treasury bond, pigs, or furniture as pledges. In Zhoujia Village, Sunfang Township in Jiangxi's Chongren County on 24 December 1988, we witnessed the following: Four sturdy men carrying a fat pig with an old man crying behind them toward the village bus station. We asked the old man what happened. He replied in a sad mood: "As I could not deliver the public grain because of disasters and could not pay 500 yuan (grain taxes evaluated in terms of money), I had to give them the pig as a pledge" (59).

The amount of grain procured in 1988 was the lowest in recent years—50 million tons or about 13 percent of total production. Why was it so difficult to procure what was by past standards a relatively small amount? Liu and Wang gave several reasons. One was that, given the price increases for farm inputs such as fertilizers and for manufactured consumer goods, peasants thought the price of grain was too low. Another was that restrictions (the exact nature of which was not specified) were imposed on the sale of grain in the markets—reportedly, counties prohibited the sale of grain outside their borders.

But perhaps the greatest source of resistance to the procurement campaign was that much of the grain was acquired *without payment being made for it*. The various procurement agencies did not have enough cash to pay for all the grain that they forced the peasants to deliver. Instead, peasants were paid with IOUs. Liu and Wang estimated that in central and western China IOUs were used to pay for 50 percent of the grain delivered. They reported that a peasant said to them, "Is it reasonable for the government to compel us to sell grain at original prices and yet not pay us?" (59). It is difficult to imagine mismanagement of the financial system to such a degree that there were not adequate funds to pay for the farm crops procured. It is not as if funds were needed for a long-term investment; after all, the crops and other products would be sold in their entirety within a year from the time procured. Basically, management of the cash flow was required.

Probably one reason for the shortfall of funds to pay farmers was that the 1989 budget for consumer price subsidies for food products was 40 billion yuan. An indication of the urban bias of the Communist party was that it did not ask the urban population to share in the cash shortfall by temporarily paying higher prices or accepting lower wage payments until there was sufficient money to pay the farmers. All of the cost of the mismanagement was imposed upon the farmers.

The problem of inadequate cash to pay for farm procurements still had not been solved by mid-1989. In May there were reports that 10 billion yuan were lacking to pay for procurements estimated to cost twice that amount (FBIS-CHI-89-093, May 16, 1989, 70). A later report (August 23, 1989, 69) noted that the shortage of funds was being handled without the issuance of a significant number of IOUs. Apparently, there was either an order from above not to issue IOUs or local officials recognized the peasants' distaste for the pieces of white paper. The solution was a very simple one: take the grain, do not pay for it, and do not issue IOUs either. It was reported that in Hunan about 18 percent of the rice delivered had not been paid for and that in some areas in Fujian "only 70 percent of the rice sold to the state has been paid [for]."

The retrogression in procurements and markets was further illustrated by the announcement in the *Farmers' Daily* in August 1989 that the price to be paid for cotton was to be increased by a substantial percentage. The price increase was accompanied, however, by the closing of the free market and the state once again asserting its monopsony power in the cotton market: "The cotton market will not be open. A double pricing system which could precipitate price hikes, panic buying, profiteering, all detriments to the state plan, will not be allowed." The consequences of this move to rural factories that make cotton textiles are likely to be disastrous.

For some time Du Runsheng has emphasized the necessity of price reform to complement the household responsibility system. In a talk given in 1985, Du (1989, 180) emphasized the need for the reform of prices. To him, this meant more than just making national price relationships more rational; it also meant the need to create "a national integrated market where operators can expect comfortable profits and circulation of products is well organized."

A national market does not exist for any agricultural product in China today. Usually, the absence of a national market stems from the shortcomings of the transportation system, but although the limitations of that system are substantial, they are not the main reason for the absence of national markets. The primary reason is bureaucratic intervention. There does not seem to be a governmental unit so small in area or importance but what it can prevent the movement of a product across its borders.

The role of bureaucratic intervention can be illustrated by a report on the reopening of grain markets in Jiangxi Province on April 1, 1989—presumably the markets had been closed since at least the fall of 1988 (FBIS-CHI-89-123, June 28, 1989). In this report there was a hint that the grain market was opened so that the procurement agencies could buy grain: "By 25 May, the grain departments purchased 100 million kg of grain at negotiated prices." Markets have value, even for bureaucrats! The same report noted that the "border grain market . . . had been strictly controlled in the past. . . . " In other words, the province controlled the outmovement of grain until the markets were reopened.

This report also substantiated the authority of counties to intervene in the grain markets: "According to some grain-producing counties, the grain markets are not yet opened in full-scale. After fulfilling purchase quotas, the peasant households of some localities cannot engage in buying and selling of grain outside the county because there are still various kinds of checkposts at the border." Thus, it will take much more than improvements in the transportation system to create a national market for agricultural products.

## CHAPTER 8

# Are the Reforms Being Lost?

In mid-1989 China's economic reforms were beset on a number of fronts. Rural industry's rapid growth was blamed for its contribution to the overheating of the economy and for its competition with state enterprises for energy and raw materials. The austerity policies introduced in late 1988 to control inflation were biased against rural areas and may cause some disruption in agricultural production. If so, this will add fuel to the firestorm of arguments that the rural reforms are no longer working because of the failure of grain production from 1985 through 1988 to exceed the 1984 level. Some of the government responses to the inflationary pressure have included the reimposition of price controls, rationing of food products, and restraints on the functioning of rural markets. For some products—cotton, for example—the market was closed down in 1989.

One of the direct consequences of the effort to limit investment expenditures has been measures to force perhaps millions of urban construction workers back to the rural areas from which they came. In fact, in Beijing in August 1989 I was told that 20 million current residents of the larger cities who had come from rural areas were to be sent back to the countryside. In terms of numbers, this would equal the mass forced exodus from the cities that occurred in 1961 and 1962. Apparently in preparation for the forced return, city residents were required as of September 1, 1989, to carry identity cards to prove that they were legal residents of the city in which they were living. The rationale for this mass movement is uncertain. In part it seems designed to cleanse the cities of certain "undesirable elements" such as many of the hawkers and traders who have come from rural areas. It may be nothing more than to once again reserve for urban residents their higher level of amenities and real incomes by prohibiting all but a select few from the countryside from sharing in the superior urban facilities. Thus, the disposal of 20 million unwelcome urban guests may not have any significant ideological foundation other than being a reflection of the all-pervasive urban bias.

## Urban Free Markets

According to the lead paragraph in a story in the *China Daily* (August 19, 1989) about the free markets in urban areas, "Today, more than 70,000 markets in China's cities are supplying its 200 million residents with more than 70 percent of their daily vegetables and half of their non-staple food." City residents bought more than 50 percent of their pork, eggs, poultry, and fish from these markets. It was reported that the value of business increased from 38.6 billion yuan in 1983 to 162 billion yuan in 1988. Not all of the expenditures were for food because free markets now deal in virtually every type of consumer goods. Since these markets play such a large role in supplying food to the urban population, it seems unlikely that, other than the threats posed by interventions associated with misguided efforts to control inflation through the imposition of price ceilings, this important segment of the reforms is in danger of being lost. Price ceilings, of course, can do a great deal of harm to how well these markets function.

## Survival of Rural Enterprises and Industries

Rural industry is frequently a scapegoat for the shortcomings of industrial development in China. The difficulties confronting state industry posed by shortfalls in the availability of energy and raw materials caused by the irrational price structure are often blamed on the rapid growth of rural industry and its claimed but never proven inefficiency.

A story in the *China Daily* (August 24, 1989) placed the blame for many of the ills of the industrial sector upon rural industry: "The industrial slowdown began at the end of 1988, because of the central government's austerity policies and economic adjustment. Nevertheless, the excessive growth of rural industry by draining supplies of energy and raw materials, is undermining attempts to co-ordinate development of the national economy. . . . " The article noted that in 1988 rural industry accounted for 25 percent of the nation's industrial output; output also grew by 30 percent in 1988 compared to the prior year and at a much higher rate than the output of state industries. In the five years ending in 1988 rural industry had a growth rate that was 22 percentage points greater than that of urban industry. Moreover, the faster growth rate of rural industry persisted into 1989. During the first five months of 1989, the output of rural industry was 24 percent greater than in the same period a year earlier, while urban industry increased its output by only 6 percent.

It is true that the demand for energy, especially for electricity, exceeds the supply at prevailing prices. In the major industrial areas of China such as Shanghai and Guangzhou, factories must close down two or three days per week because there is no electricity available. Some of the smaller rural industries, however, generate their own electricity and thus do not rely on the state electricity system.

Are these criticisms and complaints sufficient to cause a reversal of the central government's policy of benign neglect of rural industry? As noted in the previous chapter, township and village industries are supported by local authorities because such such enterprises provide the local governments with a large share of their revenue. Under the financial decentralization policies that have been followed, local governments no longer rely on the central government for all of their revenue. Thus, these governments have found it in their interest to encourage rural industries. Limiting the amount of credit available to rural industries and other enterprises is one obvious approach the central government can take to restricting the development of rural industry. But probably the most ominous and disturbing approach is to limit the access of rural industries to raw materials and energy. This seems to have already occurred with the closing down of the market for cotton, and it will probably be followed by similar actions affecting other raw materials such as wool and silkworms, if such actions have not already been taken.

### Will Rural Freedoms Be Restricted?

Another way of stating the problem is: Will the household responsibility system be emasculated? This question is raised not in the context of the events of 1989 but in response to certain concrete deviations from the household responsibility system that had already occurred. Whether or not it is national policy, political forces are acting to recentralize the power that once rested in the hands of production team and brigade leaders and the officials of the communes. In most parts of rural China it appears that the individuals who had a great deal of authority under the commune system still have a great deal of authority in the leadership of villages and townships. These groups continue to make many decisions that affect farm people, such as how delivery quotas are allocated among families, the terms under which farm inputs are to be made available, and how the incomes from village and township enterprises are distributed. The claim that the responsibility system has not solved the grain problem becomes a rationalization for such individuals and groups to seek alternative means of increasing grain production. The failure to provide the optimum circumstances for enlargement of crop operations under the responsibility system becomes an excuse for partial recollectivization of agriculture.

As the value of farm labor increases with economic growth, China will have to choose among three major alternatives (Johnson 1987). One alternative would be to follow the path chosen by Japan and later South Korea of increasing real farm prices so that farm families can earn a reasonable level of income on farms that are only slightly larger than the current ones. A second is to permit the transfer of the rights to use land—either by rental or sale—so that the land area of operating units can be enlarged over time within the framework of the household responsibility system. The third is to sanction or encourage collective forms of farming in which those activities having economies of scale are done collectively, while other activities requiring attention to detail and careful work are left to each separate family.

The first alternative of increasing farm prices significantly above world market prices is not a viable one for China. When such policies were adopted in Japan and South Korea, farm people were a minority of the total population, and the rest of the population had sufficient income to pay domestic prices that exceeded import prices. In China there is no way that the nonfarm minority of the population would pay prices high enough to make the present-sized farm units economically viable for the next decade or longer if rates of national economic growth are at 5 percent or more.

The second alternative of allowing the rental or sale of the rights to use land has been considered by researchers (Zhou Qiren 1988) and has been experimented with in some agricultural areas. The central government has not approved this approach for general adoption, however. If rental or sale of land-use rights were permitted, the average size of farm units would increase, permitting the rural areas to adapt to the increased value of labor. Equally important, permitting and encouraging the lease or sale of land-use rights would expand the freedom of rural people—the opposite of the probable outcome of encouraging collective forms of organization.

The three examples of agricultural organization that follow may reflect what is in store for China in the years ahead. It is not known, however, how typical these examples are or how likely they are to be duplicated in the future. If these different forms of agricultural organization were arrived at democratically—that is, if within a village people could freely choose how their agricultural resources were to be organized—there is nothing inherently inappropriate about any particular form of organization. But, given the power and authority held by village and township leaders in most parts of rural China, one could be skeptical about how free farm families are to choose how they wish to farm—whether to stay with the responsibility system, to accept a return to being hired workers, or to be subject to partial or full collectivization.

These examples appear to have been supported in Document No. 1, issued by the Central Committee of the Communist Party on January 1, 1986. Although this document stated that "it was imperative to adhere to integrating unified methods and decentralized ones," it provided the opening for centralized decisions:

> As there are considerable disparities in social and economic conditions in different places, the content, forms, scale and degree of combined unified with decentralized management may vary. In regions where the collectives have less accumulation, production is concentrated on similar crop[s] and intended mainly for local consumption,

> the work should start at the root to earnestly help the peasants solve their difficulties in production and circulation and steadily enrich the cooperative content. In places having well-developed economy and soundly based collective enterprises, the advantages of unified management and distribution should be used to the full, agricultural capital construction and technical transformation strengthened, operational scale appropriately adjusted and coordinated growth of agriculture, industry and commerce encouraged. (Central Committee 1986, 7)

Although the document states that the responsibility system should not be changed "at random, departing from the people's wishes," it adds that "people are dissatisfied with localities that have not undertaken tasks that one household cannot do well or at all." Within these guidelines local officials seem to have considerable room for modifying the household responsibility system.

A report on the National Rural Work Conference held in November 1988 discussed the conclusions that had been reached on improvements in the household responsibility system (FBIS-CHI-88-235, December 7, 1988). One conclusion was the need to develop socialized services "which are needed before and after production, and cannot be provided, or properly provided by a single household, such as information, technological assistance, funds, crop protection services, machines, warehouses, and circulation services" (41). These proposals seem consistent with individual responsibility. It continued:

> As for large-scale management of land, several basic points were clarified at the meeting; 1) It is conducive to raising land and labor productivity, and solving the problem of lower returns from growing grain. . . . 2) There are two prerequisites for large-scale management: Job opportunities are available for surplus labor forces, and there is a certain amount of accumulation funds. These two conditions are not found in most areas of the country at present. 3) In places where conditions are ripe, we can encourage and advocate large-scale management. But first we should proceed at an appropriate pace and engage in intensive farming. Second, we should stick to the principle of voluntary participation, not resort to coercion and commandism, and not act with undue haste. Third, we should preserve the strong points of the household contract system, and should not slip back to the old rut of allowing everyone "to eat from the same big pot."

Local officials, on reading these conclusions, can readily justify substantial increases in township or village authority over the organization of farming. Moreover, it presumably is their decision whether there is adherence to voluntary participation. Finally, everything has been done in due haste.

**Big Family.** The Big Family is a family that has been assigned land and perhaps other resources by a village or township and employs a significant number of hired workers.[5] In 1985 I visited a village near Shenyang in which there were 650 farm workers. Ten families operated small family units, using only their own labor and operating under the household responsibility system. The remaining 625 workers worked for seventeen Big Families, an average of 37 workers per farm, and received a wage plus a share of the net income. In this village in which vegetables were produced under plastic, one of the 17 Big Families operated 7.5 acres of land of which 5 acres were under plastic. This Big Family employed 52 farm workers (another Big Family in the village hired 80 workers) and also controlled a factory that employed 56 workers. In the combined farm and factory this family employed 108 workers or 7 percent of all the workers in the village. The member of this Big Family whom I met with had been the head of a production team in the immediate past. This village had given up collective agriculture only the year before.

How prevalent is the Big Family? I was told in Shenyang that 5 percent of all farmland in China was operated by Big Families. I have asked others about it, and those who had a view said that the 5 percent seemed reasonable in 1985.

**Five Unifieds.** A second example of significant collectivization of the agricultural operations—the Five Unifieds—was found in about 5 percent of the villages in Zouping County in Shandong Province as of 1987. In this approach to farming, land is assigned to each household, but five farming operations are carried out collectively: plowing, seeding, fertilizing, irrigating, and harvesting the wheat. The other crops—principally corn, cotton, and peanuts—are harvested by the households because hand labor is required. Village officials operate and control nonagricultural enterprises, including manufacturing and processing plants. The profits from these enterprises are used to subsidize certain farming operations such as plowing, irrigation, and fertilization, and to provide free fish and ducks for certain festivals or holidays. In this way, significant incentives are provided to induce the villagers to accept the incursion of collective controls in the agricultural sector—for example, the crops grown by each family are decided not by them but by the village authorities. It is not clear how satisfied the farm families are with these arrangements. Clearly, village officials have a great deal of authority stemming from their control of the nonagricultural activities and the direction of agricultural operations. It must be recognized that the Five Unifieds include operations in which there are either economies of scale, as in plowing the fields with a tractor, or the need for unity of decisions, as in operating the irrigation system. Apparently, there have been no published studies on the economic effectiveness of this system compared with that of the household responsibility system.

**Cooperative farms.** In Shunyi County in the Beijing Municipality an experiment is under way that in many ways is a return to the commune system. This county has seen rapid development of its nonagricultural employment. Its total labor force is 220,000 and was at that level throughout the 1980s. In 1980, only 20,000 were employed in township industries; in 1988, 170,000 plus 20,000 contract workers from outside were employed in those industries. County enterprises have not expanded and employ 10,000. While the majority of workers were engaged in agriculture in 1980, in 1988 only 28,000 were engaged in crop farming. The county followed the household responsibility system through 1986, and it seemed to have been quite successful. Per capita incomes increased from 140 yuan in 1978 to 859 yuan in 1984, and grain production increased by 6.4 percent annually from 1978 to 1984. Growth slowed to about 1 percent for the next two years, however. At the end of the household responsibility system, farmers were receiving most of their income from tertiary and secondary occupations—most had become part-time farmers and, as it was said, "did not have high incentive for grain production."

The reform consisted of establishing "cooperative farms" of 3,000 mu or 500 acres. The farms do not own their machinery but are served by tractor stations. How the change was made from the household responsibility system to cooperative farms was illustrated by what happened in one township. In 1987, there were 997 agricultural workers on thirty-five farms. In August 1988 a new policy was adopted, reducing the number of farms to 3 and the number of farm workers to 507. Many of the workers who left still had a year or more on their land-use rights. When asked how these farmers were induced to give up their rights, local officials said that the farm managers employed team leaders, and the team leaders employed people—the best people. The others were promised jobs in the township industries. They also said that two principles were applied in the transition to the new policies. One was that both the land and the enterprises are collectively owned; therefore one cannot occupy a job in both areas. The other was that the minority must obey the majority. What may in fact have been true was that the majority had to obey a very small minority.

How the agriculture of one township is organized indicates the degree to which the old leadership has regained its authority. Each of the sixteen natural villages in the township is represented on the township's farm committee by the village head. There are five farms in the township, and each farm has operational teams responsible for 1,000 mu. In every case the team leaders were former brigade leaders. Each of the team leaders supervises from twenty to thirty workers, who operate under a contract that relates compensation primarily to output level with little apparent recognition of costs.

It appears that in an effort to make this experiment a success, agriculture is heavily subsidized by the nonagricultural enterprises. Investment is outrageously high; investment in agriculture (not counting the value of land) is about $1,000 per acre at the official rate of exchange or about $600 at a more realistic rate. As a measure of investment in land, the $600 is about the same as the investment in buildings, machinery, and livestock plus half the value of land in Iowa. Given the large difference in labor earnings, it seems obvious that there is either too much investment in Shunyi County or too little in Iowa.

The secretary of the Communist party in this county had close contact with national leaders. In addition to his personal traits, he had two important assets. The county has a golf course that is used by national leaders, and possibly the best tailor in the Beijing Municipality has his shop in the county. Thus, the county receives frequent visits from national leaders, who are kept informed of the miraculous but undocumented results of the experiment.

The violation of property rights that occurred in Shunyi County is not unique. In an article concerned with reasons for the low rate of investment in agriculture, the insecurity of the rights to use land was indicated as one of the major impediments to investment (FBIS-CHI-89-062, April 3, 1989, 67). The particular issue addressed was that of changing the structure of farming from the individual household responsibility system to larger and collectivized modes of operation: "Peasants still have a lingering fear of a change in policy. Over the past years, some areas have frequently readjusted and merged pieces of land, and have propagated and promoted the practice of large-scale operation of land in an inappropriate way. This has intensified the peasants' worry in this respect." The "change in policy" is that peasants will have their land-use rights taken from them in an arbitrary, coercive, and undemocratic way and will be forced to participate in an agricultural organization that has many of the characteristics of the communes.

## Establishing Valid Property Rights

The issue considered in the previous section is much less about the particular form of the organization of agriculture than it is about how the decisions are made to establish a given form. The important issue is whether the form adopted is based on the voluntary participation of the participants. If such is truly the case, many different forms of economic organization can be efficient and successful. But there is evidence, such as that provided by Shunyi County, that at least some of the departures from the household responsibility system are based on coercion.

The strongest protection against arbitrary modification or seizure of land-use rights would be a clear definition of those rights, the recording of those rights in a public institution, and the establishment of a legal mechanism for protecting those rights. At the present time, use rights are neither recorded outside the ownership unit that allocates them nor clearly and specifically defined. Apparently, rights can be taken away without the consent of their owners and have been in some cases. When faced with such unattractive alternatives as not being permitted to retain the land-use rights while holding a nonfarm job, many families give up their rights.

A direct quotation from Zhou Qiren, which was only paraphrased in Chapter 7, is appropriate here:

> Property rights . . . (are) the rights to obtain returns and allocate the means of production. Therefore, [they prohibit] any behavioral main body in society (individuals, families, or enterprises) from taking things away from other behavioral main bodies. A clear definition of property rights is the foundation for division of labor and exchange. If people can easily use methods to take things away from others, nobody will spend any effort developing production which involves

> division of labor and is for carrying out exchange with others. The definition of property rights is the foundation for the social and economic orders and will promote equality in exchange. Any unwillingness to define property rights will obstruct the development of exchange, division of labor and cooperation. (FBIS-CHI-88-226, November 23, 1988, 42)

The reasons for clearly defining the property rights in the land-use rights allocated under the household responsibility system are so important and weighty that there must be another equally important reason or reasons these rights have not been established and a system created for recording and ensuring them. The most likely reason this has not occurred is that clear definition of the property rights of the farm households would greatly reduce the arbitrary power and authority of the now powerful local authorities such as secretaries of the parties at the village, township, and county levels, as well as some local governmental officials. Consequently, there are strong vested interests, who so far have been able to resist the creation of a property rights system.

The absence of well-defined property rights is also a problem in the urban economy. Many incentive problems in urban enterprises are due to the ill-defined nature of the property rights that determine how resources are allocated and how income should be divided. Industrial decentralization has failed not only because of the irrational price system, but also because those who make decisions concerning such matters as wages and bonuses have little interest in the long-run profitability of an enterprise in which their property right is so uncertain and limited. Thus, when enterprises have been given control over the distribution of the income produced, investment has been neglected in favor of larger distributions to the management and workers. Only when the property rights in industrial enterprises are well defined and those who control the property rights have an interest in maximizing their value will it be possible to give substantial autonomy to the individual enterprises. This is clearly a necessary condition, but it is not sufficient. Much more is required, including a functioning market system in which inputs can be purchased as desired and outputs sold to willing buyers.

## CHAPTER 9

# Barriers to Further Reform

This final chapter will make two main points. The first is that aside from the difficulties imposed on the rural reform effort by the macroeconomic imbalances in the economy, these reforms are being harmed by wrong analyses and conclusions about the outcomes of the reforms since 1984. The second point is that China's policy makers do not agree on what is required for a successful reform of industry. The second point is in no way peculiar to China. Each of the centrally planned economies now attempting to follow a path of reform is caught in a vacuum. While there may be general agreement on the undesirability of the present situation and the desired future state of affairs, there is a fatal absence of understanding of what steps must be taken if the desired future state of affairs is to be realized. It is quite clear that Soviet President Mikhail Gorbachev and his advisers lack such a blueprint for making the transition from the present very unsatisfactory state of affairs in the Soviet Union to the desired objective of a more productive economy that will satisfy the demands of its citizens for a variety of goods and services comparable to that in the Western European economies.

Considering the difficulties confronting the reform efforts in the Soviet Union and the limited success of Hungary's industrial reforms after nearly two decades of effort, the remarkable and rapid success of China's rural reforms is even more unusual than it appeared at the time the reforms unfolded. The reforms were associated with rapid improvement in the production of farm products and rapid and sustained growth in the real incomes of the farm population. The success of the reforms was to a considerable degree dark testimony to the inefficiency of the policies and institutions that were replaced, but it was much more than this. Presumably, alternative reform paths could have been followed with less striking results.

The success of the rural reforms was primarily due to the willingness of the government to permit rural people a wide degree of freedom in the use of their resources, accompanied by the assurance that they would receive the benefits arising from the productivity of their resources. Thus, there was a significant improvement in the security of their property right in the fruits of their labor. Of course, the rural reforms did not create a full set of freedoms, with all decisions being made in response to prices determined in the market. Labor mobility remained restricted, and the government continued to intervene in markets in a number of ways, especially by procurements of grains and other farm products and by the reimposition of price ceilings whenever market prices rose above some politically acceptable level. But by any standard that one might wish to apply, an enormous reduction in governmental intervention in the lives of the peasants occurred.

Another and generally unrecognized reason why the rural reforms moved ahead with a high level of support from policy makers and with so little resistance from the urban population was that the communes were financially self-supporting—one consequence of the urban bias of the economic development policies under Mao. Although some relief supplies of food were available when there was a serious natural disaster, the large majority of the communes generally had no claim on any resources other than their own. As a consequence, the absolute and relative prices of agricultural products had to bear some reasonable relationship to the absolute and relative costs of producing those products. The relationships were not perfect, of course, because there was coercion in purchase of farm products, but overall the income that remained had to be sufficient to cover minimal living expenditures most of the time.[6]

This was not then nor is it now the situation in industry. Some enterprises are highly profitable, and others suffer large losses. Output prices have little relationship to the underlying cost structures, and many prices have remained unchanged for long periods of time. Under the commune system farm prices were adjusted from time to time, apparently in recognition of the self-financing nature of the communes. While one of the first actions of the reforms was to increase farm procurement prices and to make some adjustments in relative prices, the price structure was not changed radically. Unfortunately, before industrial enterprises can be put on a self-financing basis—a critical component in a successful reform—far more drastic price changes will be required than was in the case for agriculture.

For reasons that may have appeared overwhelming at the time, it was decided not to pass on the increase in the prices of grains and vegetable oils to consumers; instead, the increases in the procurement prices were paid by the government. In 1979 the cost of the food subsidies seemed to be manageable, but the cost has ballooned in the years since. The food subsidies are available only to urban residents, and yet it was reported in 1988 that the cost of "the food-related subsidies [is] now almost double the country's education budget" (FBIS-CHI-88-070, April 12, 1988, 61). As was shown in Chapter 5, the average consumption level of the urban population is at least double that of the rural population, yet almost twice as much is spent on the former's food subsidies as is spent on the education of more than 100 million students in all of China, both urban and rural.

As is known from the democratic experience, when costly food price subsidies go to the highest-income segment of the national population, it is more difficult to eliminate them. In a socialist dictatorship as well as in a democratic government, this is the part of the population with the greatest political influence. The introduction of the food price subsidies has now led to a situation in which these subsidies are a major barrier to further reforms in both industry and agriculture. The subsidies are a barrier to industrial reform because of the distortion of prices and role of the food price and other subsidies in reducing the effect of wages on the incentive to work. With the increase in subsidies, a larger and larger fraction of the real income of a family is independent of the income earned from work. This is anomalous, since a primary objective of urban reforms has been to eliminate the principle of everyone eating from the same big pot and to strengthen the relationship between productivity and reward.

The food price subsidies are a serious threat to the agricultural reforms because they are a barrier to increasing the prices paid to farmers for grains and vegetable oils and other subsidized foods. A price increase requires an increase in government expenditures on food subsidies, and officials faced with a budget deficit are reluctant to increase prices paid to farmers even when output may be lagging because of a lack of incentive for the producers. As shall be seen below, the grain fetish of Chinese officials combined with the recent stagnation of grain production means that the difficulties encountered in keeping grain prices at a level adequate to call forth the desired grain supplies constitute a serious barrier to rational consideration of the rural reforms.

## Mistaken Analyses and Bad Policies

According to the highest Chinese officials and most urban intellectuals with whom I have talked, the grain problem is *the* agricultural problem. Most Chinese agricultural policy makers are obsessed with the national grain output. Until 1989 grain production had failed to equal the 1984 record. Even though total agricultural output grew at an annual rate of 4 percent from 1985 to 1988, the press has included many statements questioning whether the rural reforms, and especially the household responsibility system, were now meeting their objectives.

At the National Rural Work Conference held in November 1988 (FBIS-CHI-89-003, January 5, 1989, 23), Deng Xiaoping was quoted as having said: "In agriculture, the main problem is grain." Li Peng was also quoted: "The stable growth of agriculture, particularly grain production, is the foundation for the long-term stable development of the national economy." And Zhao Ziyang said "We must tightly grasp the grain problem." If the national leaders who made these statements followed them up with constructive actions that would result in increased grain production, their grain fundamentalism would be relatively harmless. But when such statements are made and nothing is done to address the problem they designate, their statements become implicit criticisms of the rural reforms. This is the case whether or not they intend such an interpretation.

It is distressing to hear Chinese officials with responsibility for agriculture state that the rural reforms are no longer effective. When asked how they reached this conclusion, the answer is always that grain production has not increased since 1984. When they are reminded that agricultural output has continued to grow at a high rate, their response seems to indicate that either they do not know that to be true or, if it is, it is unimportant as long as grain production is lagging.

In May 1989 I visited the Soviet Union and met with several individuals concerned with agricultural reform in their country. I often asked if consideration had been given to adopting reforms similar to the rural reforms in China. On one occasion I was told that since the Chinese rural reforms were no longer effective, there was no reason to try to learn from them. When I asked why it was believed the Chinese reforms were now ineffective, I was told that two researchers from an important Chinese institution had so informed them. As for the reason for such a conclusion, it was said that agricultural output had stagnated.

Similarly, a friend who returned from China in late September 1989 was informed by two economists in responsible positions that the rural reforms had failed because agricultural output had stagnated. There was no indication in the conversation that total agricultural output had continued to increase while grain production had not.

The keynote address at the National Rural Work Conference in December 1988 made by Tian Jiyun, vice prime minister in charge of agriculture, presented a positive view of the reforms and made realistic suggestions for carrying the reform process forward. He stated: "In my opinion, as a whole, the situation of rural reform is a good one and is basically sound" (FBIS-CHI-89-003, January 5, 1989, 25). He noted that reforms had not progressed as rapidly in recent years as in the first few years, explaining that in the early years the reforms were principally internal to agriculture and had little relation to urban areas. In recent years, however, reforms had become merged with the reforms in cities and towns, and the problems, such as those with prices, had become much more complex and were unsolvable by agriculture alone.

The obsession with grain production presumably stems from grain's continued high contribution—80–85 percent—to total human calorie consumption. This is the direct human intake and does not include the calories from grain fed to livestock and poultry. Consequently, a long-term decline in grain production per capita could present the government with some unsatisfactory choices: increased imports, increased investment in agriculture, and higher prices for grain and thus higher food subsidies.

What is the evidence that there is a serious grain problem in China? The only obvious evidence is that while grain production grew rapidly from 1978 to 1984, it has declined slightly since that time. In addition, although China had become a small net exporter of grain in 1984 and 1985, it has since had to import significant quantities on the order of 4–5 percent of total supplies.

But this emphasis on grain production since 1984 has ignored the large increase in per capita grain consumption since 1978. In 1978 per capita grain consumption was 195.5 kilograms; in 1987 it was 251.4. (SYOC 1988, 713).[7] This increase of 28 percent is really quite remarkable given that two decades of the commune system had not increased per capita consumption one gram, let alone one kilogram.

With the substantial increase in the national per capita availability of grain, I have seen no mention of the fact that urban grain consumption per capita has declined during the 1980s. In 1981 urban consumption was 145 kilograms, declining to 134 kilograms in 1987 (SYOC 1988, 718). This decline has not resulted from higher prices because the nominal price of rationed grain has not changed during the period, while the inflation-adjusted or real price has fallen by a substantial margin. The decline in grain consumption is a response to the increased consumption of other foods, especially meat, poultry, eggs, fish and shrimp, and vegetable oils. The decline in grain consumption is consistent with what one would expect at the income level achieved in recent years by Chinese urban residents. There is no grain crisis in China. If there is a crisis, it is a crisis in economic analysis or in rational thinking. By following appropriate policies within the structure of the household responsibility system, China can produce enough grain to equate supply and demand at reasonable prices. At present, the low prices of grain for urban consumers result in an uneconomic level of grain consumption, even with the rationing system.

The prices that farmers receive for grain, especially wheat and rice, are significantly lower than world market prices, especially if a realistic exchange rate is used. In 1989 farmers received about 500–600 yuan per ton for wheat and rice. At the official rate of exchange this is a price of $135–$162 per ton. Australian export prices for wheat have ranged from $130 to $200 per ton over the past two years, and Thailand's rice export price has been about $200 per ton when converted to a rough or paddy basis. At a more realistic rate of exchange of 6 yuan per dollar, the farm price is $100 per ton or less and some 30–50 percent below world market prices.

When government officials give the impression that the grain problem is acute and unlikely to be solved by continued reliance on the household responsibility system, support is provided for those who have opposed the reforms from the start. Continued emphasis on the grain problem while nothing is done to expand grain production increases the probability that the successful reforms will be gradually compromised. Changes adverse to the household responsibility system and to freedom in allocating resources in rural areas are already under way, though perhaps as much under the guise of controlling inflation as in response to the grain problem. But the return of price controls for many products and the abolition of or restraints on markets are a severe modification of the reforms. The use of force to collect grain only adds to the lack of trust that peasants have of the government and clearly interferes with the economic incentive to produce grain. One would have thought that two decades of experience in the commune system with the failure of coercion to motivate work would be given some thought. Yet there seem to be disturbing policy trends in the direction of reasserting the authority of local party and government officials over farming. Some of these trends were described in Chapter 8.

## Anomaly in the Agricultural Data

There is a major anomaly in the agricultural production data for China. As noted, the official data indicate that grain production has not increased since 1984. Annual grain production from 1985 to 1988 averaged nearly 4 percent below the record crop of 407 million tons in 1984 (SYOC 1988, 212). The production of pork, beef, and mutton, however, increased from 17.6 million tons in 1985 to 21.9 million tons in 1988 (*China Issues and Ideas* 5, 1989, 47). Meat production in 1989—produced largely from the 1988 grain and feed crop—was projected to be 23 million tons, or 31 percent more than in 1985. Where did the additional feed come from? If it did not come from unreported grain, it had to have come from other feed sources that competed with grain for land and other agricultural resources.

This apparent conflict in the data is consistent with several possibilities. One is that grain production is being underreported, perhaps to avoid greater extraction by the procurement agency. The second is that the meat production data are overestimated. The third is that farmers have emphasized the production of feeds other than grain. If either the first or the third of these possibilities is correct, it is nonsensical for Chinese officials to proclaim that there is a grain crisis and that agricultural reforms have failed. Instead of making such claims officials should carefully investigate this anomaly in the data. Only those who have access to the files of the State Statistical Bureau could undertake such an investigation.

## Industrial Reform Strategy

I have neither the wit nor the wisdom to provide a blueprint for the transition from the present structure of Chinese industry to a more efficient and productive system responsive to changes in technology, costs, and demands. In one sense, however, the design of such a blueprint seems quite simple, and there seems to be considerable agreement on what its main features should be.

One of its major features should be price reform that reflects the real costs of producing products, including not just the Marxist designation of costs but also the values of natural resources and the value of time or the interest rate. But price reform must do more than reflect costs; it also must recognize the role of demand and prices in determining the quantities of each commodity produced. It is not enough to have accurate estimates of costs; it is also necessary to know how much of a product the consumers or users, whether individuals or enterprises, are willing to pay for.

Another component of the blueprint can be described variously. One way is to say that enterprises should be self-financing—that is, an enterprise should be subject to bankruptcy if it does not take in sufficient revenue to cover its costs. Another way is to say that the property rights associated with the operation of an enterprise must be defined so that there is clear delineation of how the benefits and costs of the operation of the enterprise will be divided among those who contribute resources. Clear definition of the property rights is designed to provide incentives both to the workers to contribute in return for compensation directly related to their contribution and to the managers or owners to maximize the present value of the enterprise. By implication, definition of property rights must include the principle of self-financing; otherwise, the negative incentive of failure is lost, and inefficiency and greed will be rewarded if the government is willing to absorb enterprise losses.

Self-financing and clear definition of property rights are necessary and not sufficient conditions for an efficient and responsive socialist economic system. A socialist monopoly is at least as bad as a capitalist monopoly—and probably worse since socialist monopolies seem to be much more durable than capitalist ones. Socialist monopolies have been much more pervasive and powerful than monopolies in any modern capitalist system. For those who do not believe that, ask any

Chinese farmer who grows cotton or wheat or rice or any Soviet farmer who produces anything how much competition there is in the purchase of all or most of his farm products. Or ask the same farmers how much competition there is when they purchase farm machinery or other farm inputs. Or ask a factory operator in China how much choice he had in sources of supply of inputs before the dual price system.

The poor quality of services in the socialist economies is due not only to a lack of appropriate wage incentives but also to a lack of competition in the provision of services such as retailing, catering, repair, and sleeping accommodations. But it is not immediately obvious how competition can be introduced into a socialist system. This is not to say that it cannot be done, but doing so will require considerable thought and preparation. In some sectors, such as retailing and marketing, competition can be readily introduced by permitting private activities. China has already taken this step in rural marketing, and Hungary has done so in retail, repair services, and restaurants.

It is much more difficult, however, to devise a competitive strategy for those sectors of the socialist economies dominated by large enterprises that employ thousands of workers, unless the economy is to be an open economy with minimal interventions in international trade. In today's world the most effective protection against monopolistic practices is free or liberal trade. But if this alternative is not chosen, the creation of competitive-like conditions in some of the industrial sectors will require a great deal of thought and imagination. The solution rests on how property rights are allocated and how widely they are dispersed.

Before mid-1989 there was a lively discussion of how the property rights should be allocated to achieve a variety of objectives, including eliminating bureaucratic interference in the operation of enterprises, creating appropriate incentives for efficient use of labor and capital, and making enterprises responsive to the demands of the population. One proposal was that stock be issued and given to certain institutions, such as universities, to replace complete reliance on governmental appropriation. These institutions would then have an incentive to select management that would maximize the value of the enterprises. Another proposal was that the workers in each enterprise receive stock, although unless the stock is purchased by the workers the potential for creating a great deal of unearned wealth would be very great. A related and more equitable proposal was that stock be distributed to the public generally and that a stock market be created so that people could buy and sell stock and consolidate their holdings.

In China a more efficient economy requires substantial reform of the labor market. The current wage structure in the socialized sector fails to reward education and the acquisition of skills. The primary determinant of wages is length of service, and, although there are differences in wages by job classifications, these seem to have little relevance to prior preparation or education. A study of wage differentials as affected by experience, education, sex, and type of employer (state-owned or collective enterprise) was undertaken for Tianjin using 1984 data (Hu, Li, and Shi 1988, 89). The most important factors affecting monthly wages were years employed, being male, and working for a state enterprise rather than a collective. The average monthly wage, including bonuses, was 88 yuan. Each year of experience increased the monthly wage by 1.4 yuan, while being a male meant a wage of 9 yuan per month more than that of a female. Working for a state rather than a collective enterprise increased the monthly wage by 14.4 yuan.

Holding the above variables constant, a person with a college education received 5.9 yuan per month *less* than a person with a primary education, a person with a secondary technical education 2 yuan less, and a junior high graduate 2.5 yuan less. A person who had completed senior high received a substantial benefit—some 11.4 yuan more than the primary graduate—but the highest pay of all went to those who had less than a primary education, nearly 12 yuan more than those who had completed primary school.

The results for Tianjin are consistent with what is known about the wage and salary structure in urban China. Clearly, there is no monetary incentive for investment in education, or at least there was not in the early and mid-1980s. As the opportunities for private employment have expanded and as the number of joint ventures and collective enterprises have increased, there may have been some change in the economic returns to education, although I have not seen any data to support that conclusion.

This sketchy and incomplete outline of a blueprint for reform glosses over many points that would have to be faced by any government. Is the blueprint to be put in place all at once or gradually? What is to be done with the enterprises that are not viable and with the employees of those enterprises? Since China has operated under the assumption, until recently, that full employment has been achieved, there is no system of unemployment compensation except that of continuing to be paid by your work unit even if there is nothing to do. But if the work unit has gone bankrupt, an unemployment system must be installed, requiring major legislative and administrative efforts.

A new tax system would be required to replace the current system, which depends on a considerable degree of bureaucratic intervention in the enterprises. The present complex system is a result, at least in part, of the irrationality of the differential profitability of enterprises arising out of the erratic price structure for both outputs and inputs. But the functioning of the economy would probably improve if some significant share of the tax burden were shifted from enterprise profits to personal and commodity taxes.

There is an implication that in going to a market-oriented system the central government should give up ownership of the major means of production in the industrial sector. But if the central government retains ownership, it has the responsibility for seeing that those resources are used productively and efficiently. Society, even a socialist society, does not gain when a resource is used in a manner in which the return on that resource is nil. If the return to urban land is nil, for example, this does not show that socialism is superior to capitalism. It proves that the land is being used inefficiently and that other social costs of urban life—such as transportation, electricity distribution, and sewage disposal—are higher than what they would have been had the value of the land been maximized. Of course, urban residents who use such services are often not required to pay the true costs. Not only is there a great loss in economic efficiency, but there is likely to be a significant increase in income inequality.

Socialist economies have created many problems—some of which now seem impossible to resolve—by trying to influence the distribution of income through the pricing of products and services rather than through taxation and income transfers to particular segments of the population. Low-priced food, rents that do not cover the cost of maintenance (let alone interest and depreciation), subsidized public transport, and cheap energy have specific effects on the distribution of income and consumption. The general effect is to transfer most of the benefits to the middle and upper classes—to the workers in state enterprises, the bureaucrats, and the cadres. Thus, the people who benefit are not primarily the poor but those of average and higher incomes because they consume more food and have the connections to obtain larger and better-located housing than do the lower-income groups.

The use of prices in this way seriously distorts the use of resources without transferring benefits to the segments of the population most in need. In China almost none of the benefits have gone to the rural population, which has a much lower income level than the urban population. As noted earlier, the farm population has an income that is less than half that of the urban population, yet the farm population is excluded from the subsidies on food, urban transportation, and housing. It may be that there are people in cities who are so poor that they could not pay market prices for food, housing, and urban transportation. But there are income transfer programs that could be used to meet their needs without seriously distorting the price structure.

It is far from easy, however, to abolish the subsidies that now benefit primarily the highest-income 15–20 percent of the nation's population. These are the urban people who receive almost all of the benefits. The economic interests that Dong Fureng identified (see Chapter 4) that have a great deal to gain from the existing system of subsidies are extremely powerful interests in the Chinese economy. These interests may resist strongly the efforts to rationalize the price of food, housing, and transportation, even if in the long run they would be better off by eliminating the enormous inefficiencies that are now created by the subsidies.

# Notes

1. "On Questions of Party History" can be found in part or in its entirety in various places, including in the *Beijing Review* and in Liu and Wu (1986, 578–636).

2. These were that China should follow, without exception, whatever policy decisions Chairman Mao had given and "should follow without fail, from first to last, whatever directives Chairman Mao had given" (Liu and Wu 1986, 430).

3. By including only the income derived from material production, the Western concept of national income is probably underestimated by 6–7 percent. As of 1983, 6.7 percent of the total labor force in China was counted as being in the nonproductive spheres (SYOC 1984, 108).

4. An approximate rather than actual figure is given because in 1985 the construction bank was consolidated with the banking system, and actual data on the construction bank's loans were only available for the end of 1985, not the end of 1984. The actual deposits, excluding those of the construction bank, at the end of 1984 were 442 billion yuan (SYOC 1988, 687).

5. The Big Family was recognized as an acceptable form of organization in Document No. 1, *Circular of the Central Committee of the Communist Party of China Covering the Rural Work in 1984* (January 1, 1984). Available in Liu and Wu 1986, 637–55.

6. Obviously, this condition did not prevail in many rural areas in China during the great famine of 1958–1961 or during other famine periods, but the general principle that the communes were expected to be self-supporting was starkly supported during such periods.

7. The figures given are for actual human consumption; in 1978 grain production per capita was 316 kilograms. Seed, feed, industrial uses, and waste account for the difference.

# References

Three sources of data and information—two statistical yearbook series and a translation service—merit special notice. In most cases, references to material translated from the Chinese are to the publications that contain the translations rather than to the original sources.

The following citations have been used in the text for these sources:

CAY He Kang, ed. 1985, 1986, 1987. *China Agriculture Yearbook*. Engl. ed. Beijing: Agriculture Publishing House.

FBIS Foreign Broadcast Information Service. *Daily Report: China*. Springfield, Va.: National Technical Information Service, U.S. Department of Commerce.

SYOC State Statistical Bureau. 1984, 1986, 1987, 1988. *Statistical Yearbook of China* or *China Statistical Yearbook*. Beijing: China Statistical Information and Consultancy Centre.

## Other References

Ashton, B., K. Hill, A. Piazza, and R. Zeitz. 1984. "Famine in China." *Population and Development Review* 10, no. 4 (December).

Beijing Review. 1989. *China: Issues and Ideas (5)—A Decade of Reform (1979–1988)*. Beijing: Beijing Review Press.

Central Committee of the Communist Party of China. 1984. *China's Economic Structure Reform—Decision of the CPC Central Committee (October 1984)*. Beijing: Foreign Languages Press.

———. 1986. *On Arrangements for Rural Work in 1986 by the Central Committee of the CPC and the State Council of the PRC*. Document No. 1, 1986. Beijing: International Liaison Department, Research Centre for Rural Development of the PRC (also in *China Agricultural Yearbook*, 1986, 1–7).

Chow, Gregory C. 1985. *The Chinese Economy*. Cambridge, Mass.: Harper and Row.

Crook, Frederick. 1988. *Agricultural Statistics of the People's Republic of China, 1949–86*. Statistical Bulletin no. 764. Economic Research Service, U.S. Department of Agriculture.

Dong Fureng. 1982. "Relationship between Accumulation and Consumption." In *China's Search for Economic Growth: The Chinese Economy since 1949,* ed. Xu Dixin et al. Beijing: New World Press.

Du Runsheng. 1989. *China's Rural Economic Reform: Many People, Little Land.* Beijing: Foreign Languages Press.

Economic Research Service, U.S. Department of Agriculture. Annual series. *China Agriculture and Trade Report.* Washington, D.C. Formerly published under the title *China Situation and Outlook Report.*

Griffin, Keith, and Kimberly Griffin. 1985. "Institutional Change and Income Distribution in the Chinese Countryside." In *Development and Income Distribution in China,* ed. Chi Keung Leung and Joseph C. H. Chai. Hong Kong: University of Hong Kong.

Harding, Harry. 1987. *China's Second Revolution: Reform after Mao.* Washington, D.C.: Brookings.

Hu Teh-Wei, Li Ming, and Shi Shuzhong. 1988. "Analysis of Wages and Bonus Payments among Tianjin Urban Workers." *China Quarterly,* no. 113 (March), 77–93.

Johnson, D. Gale. 1987. "Agricultural Policy Reforms in the USSR and the People's Republic of China." Paper no. 87:28. Office of Agricultural Economics Research, University of Chicago, December 2, 1987.

———. 1990. *World Agriculture in Disarray.* Rev. ed., chap. 8. In press, London: Macmillan.

Korzec, Michael "Contract Labor, The Right to Work and New Labor Laws in the People's Republic of China." *Comparative Economic Studies* 30 (2), 117–49.

Liang Wensen. 1982. "Balanced Development of Industry and Agriculture." In *China's Search for Economic Growth: The Chinese Economy since 1949,* ed. Xu Dixin et al. Beijing: New World Press.

Lin Justin Yifu. 1986. "Measuring the Impacts of the Household Responsibility System on China's Agricultural Production." Department of Economics, University of Chicago.

———. 1987a. "Household Farm, Cooperative Farm, and Efficiency: Evidence from Rural De-Collectivization in China." Working Paper no. 503. Economic Growth Center, Yale University.

———. 1987b. "The Household Responsibility System Reform in China: A Peasant's Institutional Choice." *American Journal of Agricultural Economics* 69 (2), 410–15.

———. 1988. "The Household Responsibility System in China's Agricultural Reform: A Theoretical and Empirical Study." *Economic Development and Cultural Change* 36 (3) Supplement, S199–S224.

———. 1990. "Collectivization and China's Agricultural Crisis in 1959–61." *Journal of Political Economy* 98 (6).

Liu Suinian and Wu Qungan. 1986. *China's Socialist Economy: An Outline History (1949–1984).* Beijing: Beijing Review Press.

McMillan, John, John Whalley, and Li Jing Zu. 1989. "The Impact of China's Economic Reforms on Agricultural Productivity Growth." *Journal of Political Economy* 97 (4), 781–807.

Naughton, Barry. 1985. "False Starts and Second Wind: Financial Reforms in China's Industrial Systems." In *The Political Economy of Reform in Post-Mao China,* ed. Elizabeth J. Perry and Christine Wong. Cambridge, Mass.: Council on East Asian Studies of Harvard University.

Piazza, Alan. 1986. *Food Consumption and Nutritional Status in the PRC*. Boulder, Colo.: Westview Press.

Selden, Mark. 1980. "Wugong Yesterday and Today," State University of New York, Binghamton, unpublished paper.

Taubman, Wolfgang. 1985. "Problems of Urban Housing in China" In *Development and Income Distribution in China*, ed. Chi Keung Leung and Joseph C. H. Chai. Hong Kong: University of Hong Kong.

van Binneken, Wouter. 1988. "Employment and Labour Income Trends in China (1978–1986)." In *Trends in Employment and Labour Incomes: Case Studies of Developing Countries*, ed. Wouter van Binneken. Geneva: International Labour Office.

Walker, Kenneth R. 1984. *Food Grain Procurement and Consumption in China*. London: Cambridge University Press.

Wang Bingquian. 1980. Speech by the minister of finance reported in *Main Documents of the Third Session of the Fifth People's Congress*. Beijing: Foreign Languages Press.

Wen Guanzhong James. 1989. "The Current Tenure System and Its Impact on Long-Term Performance of the Farming Sector: The Case of Modern China." Ph.D. diss., Department of Economics, University of Chicago.

World Bank. 1983. *China: Socialist Economic Development. The Main Report*. Washington, D.C.: World Bank.

———. 1985. *China: Long-Term Development Issues and Options*. A World Bank Country Economic Report. Baltimore, Md.: Johns Hopkins University Press.

Xue Muqiao. 1981. *China's Socialist Economy*. Beijing: Foreign Languages Press.

———. 1986. *China's Socialist Economy*. 2d ed. Beijing: Foreign Languages Press.

Zhou Qiren. 1988. "Land System: Valid Property Rights, Long-Term Tenancy, and Paid Transfer." FBIS-CHI-88-226, November 23, 41–46.

# About the Author

D. Gale Johnson is the Eliakim Hastings Moore Distinguished Service Professor of Economics, Emeritus, at the University of Chicago, where he has been on the faculty since 1944. His distinguished career at the university has included serving as dean of the Division of Social Sciences (1960–1970), chairman of the Department of Economics (1971–1975 and 1980–1984), and provost (1975–1980).

In addition to his work at the university, Johnson has served as an economist for the Office of Price Administration, the Department of State, and the Department of the Army and was twice elected president of the National Opinion Research Center. He has been a consultant to the Rand Corporation, the Agency for International Development, the U.S. Council on International Economic Policy, and the National Academy of Sciences and the agricultural adviser to the Office of the President's Special Representative for Trade Negotiations. He is a member of the American Economic Association and of the American Agricultural Economic Association, which he served as president. Currently, while continuing to teach at the University of Chicago, he serves as chairman of the Council of Academic Advisers of the American Enterprise Institute and as editor of the journal *Economic Development and Cultural Change.*

Among his many publications are *World Food Problems and Prospects* (1976), *The Soviet Impact on World Grain Trade* (1977), *Food and Agricultural Policy for the 1980s* (1981), *Progress of Economic Reform in the People's Republic of China* (1982), *Agricultural Policy and Trade* (1985), and *Population Growth and Economic Development* (editor, with R. D. Lee, 1987).